HOW TO HOLD
A GARAGE SALE

HOW TO HOLD A GARAGE SALE

BY JAMES MICHAEL ULLMAN

Rand McNally & Company
Chicago · New York · San Francisco

Dedication

To those untold millions who, since time began and
in all languages, have ventured into the thriving
market in household goods by posting that magic
"SALE" sign at their residence.

Contents

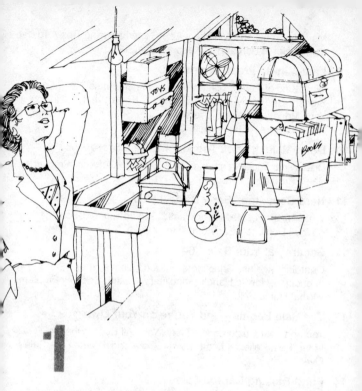

You Don't Really Need a Garage

You don't need a garage to hold a garage sale. When people talk about a "garage sale," they really mean any sale in which you use your house, apartment, or any part of the property where you live as your "store."

And so in this book "garage sale" can also mean "house sale," "basement sale," "sidewalk sale," "porch sale," "patio sale," "breezeway sale," "yard sale," "moving sale," "apartment sale," "rummage sale," "tag sale," "residue sale," "junque sale," or any other name that you think best describes what you plan to do.

In fact, many sellers simply put up signs reading "SALE."

From obscure beginnings, these sales have become a weekend institution across the country.

They have developed a loyal and sometimes fanatic following of buyers. And they give sellers a way to get cash for no-longer-wanted household goods—even to resell some at a profit.

Usually the items offered at these sales are used household goods. But they may also include antiques, works of art, and "collectibles." Some sellers offer new merchandise obtained from the businesses where they work or from auctions, bankruptcy sales, and similar outlets.

A few sellers are full- or part-time dealers moving merchandise through their own homes, or sometimes from homes, apartments, or garages rented especially for the occasion. But the vast majority are amateurs, many of them holding sales for the first time.

Whom This Book Can Help

This book is based on the experiences of many successful house and garage sellers, as well as on interviews with flea market sellers, antique dealers, and others who sell secondhand goods.

It will be especially helpful to first-time sellers, but most people who have held these sales before should also find here suggestions that will make their next sale more profitable.

It also discusses the special problems and opportunities of small groups and organizations planning to hold one of these sales to raise funds.

And it has advice for people thinking of going beyond the usual "housecleaning" motive for holding these sales, who wish to sell some items purely for profit. This involves learning to be a smart buyer of things to resell—and learning where to find them.

Forces Behind the Trend

If you're thinking of holding a house or garage sale or one of the many variations, you have plenty of company. These sales are found in virtually all communities today, but they are especially numerous in small towns, suburbs, and residential city neighborhoods. Homes and apartments in those places are usually larger, it's easier for buyers to park, and security is less of a problem than in many high-density neighborhoods.

While house and garage sales have been around for a long time, their major expansion began in the late 1960s. In those years, inflation began to soar. And as living costs continued to mount through the 1970s and into the 1980s, house and garage sales became more and more popular.

One reason is that rising prices and shrinking purchasing power are causing people to be constantly on the lookout for ways to increase their incomes. More men moonlight, more women work, and more people try to raise extra cash by selling discarded household goods rather than throwing or giving them away.

Inflation also partly explains the growing numbers of garage sale buyers. Rising living costs and mounting concern about how to get the most for their money are prompting more people to seek out bargains.

And theoretically, at least, where could you find better bargains than at a garage sale? The homeowner who needs a shovel can dig a hole just as deep with one bought for 50¢ at a garage sale as he can with a new store-bought shovel costing $6 or $7; and parents with many children can save plenty by scouring these sales for used clothing and toys.

The "Junque Market" Pyramid

Another reason for the growth of house and garage sales is that they are part of the mushrooming "junque market"—"junque" being a catchall phrase covering collectibles, antiques, and other things people buy and save for one reason or another. This market is structured like a pyramid. Garage and house sales are near the base, along with thrift shops, and slightly above scavenging for cast-offs in alleys and garbage dumps.

From there, the more desirable merchandise filters up to flea markets, to country sales and small auctions, and then up to antique shops and shows. Finally, the very best pieces find their way to major antique dealers, auctions, and collectors.

No matter what your motive for selling, when you hold a sale you become part of this market. You will probably be visited by collectors and at least a few dealers, "pickers" (people who regularly buy items for resale to dealers), and others involved in the junque trade.

And inflation has added more fuel to the growing interest in collectibles. Because of inflation, some people now view the junque they buy at house and garage sales as "investments," just as other people view stocks and bonds.

Collectors are the backbone of the junque market. But still other people go to house and garage sales seeking artifacts and mementos of bygone days for emotional reasons—the so-called nostalgia kick. Other people admire and seek older items simply because the materials and craftsmanship cannot be replicated today.

Finally, some people find an emotional release simply in going to these sales as an activity pursued for its own sake. These people— the hard-core garage sale buffs and junque addicts—are so hooked on these sales that they'll buy anything if the price seems right.

What Is a "Successful" Sale?

People hold these sales for many reasons. Some people are moving but don't want to take all of their possessions with them. Others are breaking up households, and still others hold sales once or twice a year just to clean out attics, closets, or basements.

Other people combine the "housekeeping" motive with the desire to make a profit, to one degree or another, on some of the things they sell. And a few hope to make a profit on everything. In effect, no matter what their main sources of income, these people are also semiprofessional junque dealers.

Sales are also held by community groups to raise funds. The garage sale can be to the Cub Scout troop what the rummage sale is to the church.

Given these many reasons for holding a sale, a sale that is "successful" for one person may not be a success for another.

If you're moving, almost any price would be better than being stuck with an unsold item when the sale is over. But if you're trying to sell at a profit, your price may be influenced by what *you* paid for the item. If you're not concerned with making a profit, it will be much easier to have a "successful" sale than otherwise.

The regulars who haunt house and garage sales include some of the world's most dollar-wise shoppers. Many have been studying their markets for years. Turning a consistent profit when selling to them is not easy.

How Much Can You Make?

The big question asked by everyone thinking of holding a house or garage sale for the first time is: How much will I get out of it? Again, it all depends. The variables include what you have to sell, where you live, the weather on the day or days of your sale, and how wisely (or unwisely) you plan and handle your sale and price your merchandise.

In researching this book, my wife and I have met sellers who claimed to have sold up to a thousand dollars' worth and more in sales running from a few days to a week. These people were selling fine furniture, appliances in good condition, and perhaps a few objects of art, and they were disposing of practically everything in their house.

We've also talked to housewives who had put out a few worn articles of clothing, some battered toys, and nondescript household bric-a-brac and cleared just $40 or $50 over a similar span. Still, this would be satisfactory if it provided some extra spending money in exchange for useless junk.

Generally speaking, if you live where garage sales have developed a good following, if you have a wide selection of things to sell and price your merchandise realistically, you should average from $50 to $100 per day in a sale running from two to three days. If you're moving and disposing of practically everything, you should expect to do much better than that.

2

Should You Hold a Sale?

Before you hold a sale, take a moment to be sure it will be the best way to dispose of the things you want to sell. The factors to consider are the sale's location, your ability to hold it, your attitude toward meeting the public, what you have to sell, and the alternatives available to you.

Is the Location All Right?

You won't want to hold a sale if your location is such that you would be concerned about the safety of opening your home or apartment to strangers. You might also be better off disposing of what you want to sell in some other way if the location is remote and few people would be likely to travel to it, or if parking or traffic problems would make it difficult for people to get to your sale.

In judging location, also consider your neighbors. Usually this is no problem, especially if your neighbors hold these sales too. But there could be circumstances where a sale would create parking or traffic problems that might work a special hardship on one or more neighbors. And if you live where these sales are not common, how would your neighbors feel about your holding one? Some might disapprove. Whether this matters depends on how important it is to you to keep your neighbors happy. If this is important, sound them out. To make them look more favorably on your plans, you might offer to let them put a few things of their own in your sale.

Can You Handle It?

For many people, holding a house or garage sale is a pleasant experience, but it can also be a lot of work. There's physical work in moving merchandise around in your house, garage, or whatever—and perhaps carrying it up or down stairs or in and out of attics. In addition, ads must be written and placed, signs made and put up. Someone must decide what to sell and what to charge; merchandise must be tagged and set out for display, and someone must mind the store during the sale.

As discussed in more detail later, most people holding these sales need all the help they can get from others—from their family, friends, or neighbors.

If you can't handle a sale alone and don't have any sources of help, you should think about disposing of your merchandise in some other way.

Can You Meet the Public?

When you hold a house or garage sale, you must meet the public in a selling situation. If you naturally like meeting people, you'll enjoy doing this, even though at its worst it could be like clerking at a crowded bargain-basement sale.

You'll have to cope with strangers who will want to haggle. Most of them will be polite, but within your hearing some may make insulting remarks about your prices, your merchandise, or even your housekeeping. At times you may have to deal with several people trying to talk to you at once. Children will paw through your merchandise and run through the sale area unattended. There's also the remote but ever-present possibility, discussed in Chapter 12, that you may have to cope with shoplifters.

And "meeting the public" means just that—people from all walks of life, communities, and backgrounds. When you advertise your sale, you invite everyone who hears or reads about it to attend. This won't deter most sellers. But if you are a very retiring person or would be uncomfortable in any of these situations, you may also be better off selling in some other manner.

Do You Have the Right Things to Sell?

Virtually anything in a home can be sold at a house or garage sale. In fact, these sales are the best way to dispose of the usual run of used household goods and inexpensive bric-a-brac. You'll get prices much higher than any dealer will pay. But before you hold a sale, be sure you have enough to sell to make it worthwhile in relation to the time and effort.

On the other hand, if you're trying to sell valuable antiques, collector's items, or art objects, you probably won't get top prices for many of them at a garage sale. It might be wiser for you to keep some or all of those items out of your sale while at least looking into the possibility of disposing of them through some other outlet.

What Are Your Alternatives?

While selling at your own sale probably is the most convenient and practical way for you to dispose of household items and junque, you may wish to consider these alternatives:

Paying someone to hold a sale for you. Some people are in the business of conducting house and garage sales for other people. For a commission, usually one quarter to one third of the proceeds, they will price and display your merchandise and handle all details of the sale. To learn if there are any professional sale managers in your community, you could ask the classified advertising manager of the local newspaper that runs the most garage sale ads.

If you're selling many things and don't want to be burdened with the work involved, this may be your best solution. But check with people who have dealt with the selling group to see if they were satisfied.

Selling directly to dealers. Dealers pay far below market, but for really valuable items you might not even do that well at your own sale. And if you sell everything to a dealer, at least you eliminate the time and expense of holding a sale.

Selling on consignment through a dealer. Some dealers accept better quality pieces on consignment. Terms vary, so try to compare. Selling on consignment should net you more than selling to the dealer. But be sure of the dealer's integrity—and have a clear understanding of how and when you are to be paid for the items that are sold.

Selling at an auction. This is always a gamble, but you could wind up with much higher prices here than at consignment sales. You should make sure that the auctioneer or auction house has a following, and that the following is accustomed to buying the kind of things you want to sell.

Selling directly to collectors. For most people, this is impractical. It requires that you become at least a semiprofessional dealer, spending time and money cultivating the collector market through collector publications and clubs. Unless you have relatively expensive things to sell, it won't pay. But collectors do pay the highest prices—if you can find them.

Selling at flea markets. Apart from holding their own sale, the only other way most people can sell their household junque themselves is at a flea market.

Flea Market Pros and Cons

There are many similarities between selling at garage sales and selling at flea markets. Generally speaking, though, you can charge higher prices at a flea market, where there are far more potential purchasers, than at your home. Another advantage of selling at a flea market is that you don't have to allow strangers into your home. But before making this decision, find out what special restrictions and requirements—licensing, for instance—are placed on flea market sellers. In some states sales tax will be collected from you on the spot.

In addition, three major differences between selling at garage sales and selling at flea markets may figure in your decision. First, at a flea market you're limited in what you can sell by what you can fit in the vehicle that will take you there. If you have many items, including some furniture, you may not be able to get everything to the site, and some things may be damaged in transit. Second, you don't have complete control over your sale area. In fact, you may not know how much space you have until you get there. Third—and this can be underestimated by people who have never sold at flea markets—you may have to do a lot of hard physical work in a short period of time. You must load your vehicle at your house or apartment, unload it at the market, reload unsold goods at the end of the day, and unload again when you get home. And when at the market you may also have to carry everything from a parking area to your selling space and then back again. If you're not up to all that physical activity, flea markets are not for you.

3

The Two Most Important Things You Must Know

Once you decide to hold your own house or garage sale, you should start thinking of yourself as a store. These sales are in many ways minuscule versions of retail discount store operations. For the most part, they are self-service. Usually people select merchandise, bring it to the checkout counter, and pay for it there, but occasionally a customer asks the "clerk" (you) for help.

Beyond this, to do the most effective job, sellers at garage sales must address such typical retailing problems as market research, advertising, sales promotion, pricing, merchandise display, credit, and store security.

And just as big retailers study their competitors, you can vastly increase your chances of success by following rules based on what more experienced sellers have learned. These rules stem from two essential factors:

An understanding of why people go to garage sales

An understanding of what happens at a typical sale

If you have never held a house or garage sale before, these are the two most important things you will learn from this book.

Who Will Be at Your Sale?

In one sense, the people who come to your sale will be prompted by a wide range of motives. It's impossible to categorize them all, but among the major groups are:

Your friends, relatives, and neighbors. Because they know you, many will be among your best customers.

Ordinary shoppers. Some will be looking for specific household items for which they have an immediate use, and some will be looking for any household item for which they think they may have a use sooner or later.

Junque addicts and garage sale buffs. These people haunt house sales, flea markets, auctions, etc., because they are addicted to buying junque.

Collectors. Many, but not all, collectors are also junque addicts. What distinguishes the collector is his or her specialization. Collectors know in detail nearly all there is to know about their subject, including rock-bottom prices. But if they see something they really want, they will pay a fair top price.

Dealers. They may not identify themselves, but at least a few of your customers will probably be junk or antique dealers. Usually they come at the beginning, hoping to find unrecognized treasures, or at the end, hoping to sweep up what's left for practically nothing.

Bored people. These people go to garage sales primarily to have something to do. In time they may become junque addicts. Meanwhile, they'll do more looking than buying.

No matter how varied these people's motives are in one sense, in another sense they'll all come to your sale for the same reason: They're looking for bargains. This is the common thread linking all buyers at house and garage sales. Otherwise these people wouldn't be poking around in your garage; they'd be shopping in stores.

In fact, many garage sale buffs will buy anything if they think the price is right, even if they have no immediate use for it. Either they plan to put it to use "some day," or they hope to resell the item at a higher price, perhaps at their own garage sale.

An appreciation of this is crucial if you are to make the most of your sale. It means you must provide as many bargains as you can and make it known that these bargains exist.

The "First Day" Phenomenon

You must know one other thing if your sale is to be as successful as possible:

No matter how long you run it, the first few hours will probably be the most important. You'll probably have more potential customers and sell more merchandise during this period than during the remainder of the sale.

There are exceptions to this rule, especially in sparsely populated areas where buyers must travel long distances. Your opening-hour traffic may also be held down by stormy weather, inadequate advertising and promotion, a bad starting time, or an unusually large number of other sales starting on the same day. But certainly most sellers in relatively populous areas where the garage sale has a following of buyers can anticipate that their heaviest traffic will be at the outset. All things being equal, people who attend these sales regularly want to go to sales beginning that day, and want to get there as early as possible. They believe that if a sale has been running for a while, the biggest bargains have already been snatched up. They hope to see what you have before anyone else does.

Pace of a Typical Sale

Let's say you're planning a two-day sale to run Friday and Saturday. Typically, your sale would be paced something like this:

Friday. You've announced the opening time for 9:30 a.m., but the first buyers arrive early. From 8:30 or so on, traffic will be very heavy until about 11 a.m. and will continue fairly heavy until noon, when mothers must be home to prepare meals for their children. During the afternoon the pace will be less hectic but steady.

Saturday. Only one or two buyers trickle in at the opening. Nevertheless there will be a slow, steady stream of people turning up during the day. A few of the customers will be people who were at the sale Friday and are returning for another look around. If you question your customers, you'll learn that a surprising proportion of your second-day visitors are casual passers-by attracted by signs posted on the street.

What This Means to You

The most important thing this means to you is that you must allow plenty of time in which to get ready. This can't be overemphasized.

The most common mistake made by people holding these sales is not being ready when the sale begins.

Some items are not tagged; many sellers don't even have all of their merchandise out where potential buyers can see it. And as more and more visitors tramp through the sale area, pawing through merchandise and asking questions, these sellers fall further and further behind.

There are many good reasons for being ready when the sale starts. If you are not ready, many would-be buyers will leave before they've had a chance to see everything you want to sell, and you'll lose other sales because you didn't have merchandise tagged, or you quoted too high a price off the top of your head. You also risk selling things for far less than they're worth if you have to quote prices off the top of your head.

To summarize: In planning your sale, allow plenty of time for preparations. If you're not ready when the sale begins, you won't be able to take full advantage of what are potentially your most productive selling hours.

4

The First Step:
Market Research

If you've never held a garage sale before, you should begin by doing some market research. In fact, even if you have held some sales, the more you research your market the more successful your future sales will be.

All successful retailers spend time and money studying their markets, and so should you. This book can give you general rules, but they must be modified by local conditions and practices.

Check the Laws

Talk to people who have held sales, and phone or visit your city or village officials to learn if any local laws will affect you. In most cases, none will apply. But a growing number of communities have laws that limit the number and duration of garage or house sales you can hold during a year. There may also be restrictions on the placement of signs advertising your sale.

In addition, certain items may be subject to laws and regulations. Be sure to check local, state, and federal laws before trying to sell firearms, ammunition, or explosives. Other local ordinances may cover the sale of such things as bedding, certain types of clothing, and food. Some communities may also require that you apply for a permit to hold a sale.

A few communities ban these sales altogether. Usually this happens when a few greedy people abuse the privilege and hold sales week after week, turning their homes or garages into unlicensed stores. Occasionally antique or junk dealers have tried to avoid license fees or other restrictions by marketing their wares through their homes or through homes rented from others.

Laws banning these sales do exist, usually the result of pressure on lawmakers from local merchants who don't like the competition.

Visit Other Sales

Much of your market research should involve visiting other sales in your area for the purposes of:

Seeing how others do it. The more sales you attend as a customer, the better you'll be able to plan your own sale. Seeing other people's sales will give you ideas on such things as where in your home or apartment to hold your sale, how and where to place signs, and how to display merchandise. More important, it gives you the customer's perspective. You'll soon learn what you personally like or dislike about the way some sales are held. What you like, other people will probably like too.

Checking local price levels. Many items offered at these sales will be similar, or even identical, to items you plan to sell. See what your neighbors are asking for those items. More important, try to learn if people are actually paying those prices. The world of the garage sale is a pricing jungle. Some sellers want too much for what they're selling; other sellers don't want enough. Some have firm prices, but others will lower their prices substantially for anyone who makes an offer or even shows interest.

A word of warning: When you point to an unmarked item and ask its price, you may be asked in return: "What will you give me for it?" This evasion of your question is an unfair selling tactic. Anyone selling something is obliged to quote a price as a starting point, even if he or she is willing to reduce it later. If someone tries to do this to you, say something polite and get out fast before you find you've bought something you may not want for a lot more than it's worth. And *never* use this selling tactic at your own sales.

Questioning holders of successful sales. The best local advice on how to hold your sale will come from people who have held successful sales of their own. When doing your market research, look especially for sales that seem to be going well. Then strike up a conversation with the person running the sale. Tell the seller you plan to hold a sale of your own, and see how much you can learn. Usually, if approached cordially, people will be glad to share their knowledge with you.

But don't pester people with questions when they're busy selling to customers. If necessary, come back at the end of the sale when your source will have more time to talk. A good question to ask is what they'd do differently if they had it to do all over again.

Is It Junk or Junque?

If you plan to sell household items and the bric-a-brac gathering dust in your attic, closets, or basement, you should also visit some antique stores and shows, resale shops, flea markets, and perhaps some antique auctions. This is to learn if some of the junk you plan to sell is actually junque—that is, something sought by antique buffs and collectors.

An item doesn't have to be a century old—one definition of an antique—to be wanted. If it's what the trade calls a "collectible," there could be a big demand for it. There are collectors of an infinite variety of things; some items were mass-produced and widely distributed in their time, and others are handcrafted, one-of-a-kind pieces. Generally speaking, the items most in demand are those no longer being produced that have a touch of "Americana" about them.

For economic reasons, the number of things being collected is expanding rapidly. The prices of many traditional antiques and collector's items have been bid up so high that only the most affluent can now afford them. This induces people with collecting instincts but more modest budgets to seek different and less expensive things to collect. And of course the "nostalgia kick" is driving many people to start buying mementos of yesteryear.

Major "Collectible" Categories

So many items are now sought by collectors that no one book could even catalog them all, although several have tried. If you visit one of the larger antique shows, you'll see some of the myriad books published on various categories of collecting.

Some of the major categories are:

Advertising
Automobiles and
   accessories
Banks
Barbed wire
Bells
Books
Bottles
Brassware
"Breweriana"
Buttons and badges
Carnival glass
China and crystal
Clocks and watches
Coins and stamps
Copperware
Depression glass
Doll furniture
Dolls
Farm items
Furniture
Gambling devices
Gems and minerals
Indian relics
Inkwells
Insulators
Jewelry
Lamps
Locks and keys

Magazines
Military items
Miniatures
Objects from Occupied
   Japan
Phonograph records
Photographic
   equipment
Plates
Pocketknives
Political campaign
   souvenirs
Postcards
Pottery
Primitive arts and crafts
Prints, pictures,
   paintings
Quilts
Radio memorabilia
Railroad artifacts
Razors, shaving mugs
Sheet music
Souvenir plates,
   spoons, etc.
Sports mementos
Tools
Toys
Weapons
World's Fair souvenirs

Special Advice for Senior Citizens

The people most likely to sell collectibles for far less than they are worth are senior citizens. Probably that's because it's not easy to realize that items once so commonplace as to be virtually worthless in your youth or middle age now have value as antiques.

Older couples preparing to move and elderly widows and widowers breaking up their households often let collectibles go for a fraction of their market value. You people should make it a point to research the antique and junque markets to be sure you don't have unrecognized treasures. If you can't do it yourselves, have a relative or friend do it for you.

Of course, your visits to antique shops may disclose that your household junk is indeed what you first thought it to be—junk. You may also find that even though some of your junk is junque, it is low-priced junque. On the other hand, you may be pleasantly surprised to find high prices on some things you first thought were worthless.

How Much Research Is Enough?

How much research you should do depends on what you have to sell and how much time you can spend.

But you should resign yourself to the fact that there's no way you can give yourself a crash course that will make you an expert in antique and collectible values in a few weeks, months, or even years.

The field is so vast that you can spend a lifetime in the trade and still be truly expert in only relatively few fields. The best you can do over a short period of time is to be sure you don't seriously underprice relatively valuable items, or sell truly valuable pieces for virtually nothing.

Sources of Information

Countless books on antiques and collectibles have been published. Your public library may have many of them, and its reference department may even have one or more general price guides to antiques and collectibles.

If you live in or near a city, you may also have access to a news agency that sells some of the major periodicals in the antique and collectible field. Sometimes these periodicals are also sold at antique shows and flea markets.

In addition to general price guides, there are specialized guides to thousands of categories of collector's items. A good price guide can help by warning you when prices are unreasonably high or low. Used intelligently, these sources are valuable tools, but they have major limitations. They cannot reflect rapid price changes or geographic price differences; they cannot take into account the infinite variations in the condition of collectibles, nor can they possibly include everything. Also, the people compiling these guides occasionally make mistakes.

Consequently, the best "guide" to the price of an item is the current market—what the people where you plan to sell it are willing to pay at the time you are selling it.

There are many collector and antique publications and price guides on the market. Some of the best periodicals are:

Antique Trader Weekly, P.O. Box 1050, Dubuque, IA 52001

Collectors News, 606 Eighth Avenue, Grundy City, IA 50638

Hobbies, 1006 S. Michigan Avenue, Chicago, IL 60605

Among the most useful price guides are:

Antiques and Their Prices, Edwin G. Warman, Warman Publishing Company, Inc., 540 Morgantown Road, Uniontown, PA 15401

Antique Trader Quarterly Price Guide to Antiques and Collectibles, P.O. Box 1050, Dubuque, IA 52001

Kovel's Complete Antique Price List, Crown Publishers, Inc., New York, NY 10016

Organizing Your Sale

Before you get very far with plans for your garage sale, you'll have to make some basic decisions. In part they'll be determined by your market research, but they may also be determined to some extent by circumstances beyond your control.

Where Will You Hold It?

All other things being equal, it's a lot easier to hold a sale if you live in a house rather than an apartment. But wherever you hold it, the "sale" area should be clearly set off from all other areas. Ideally there should be unmistakable barriers between the sale and nonsale areas. A garage sale proper is a good example of this. Everything for sale is displayed in the garage (and perhaps on the lawn and/or driveway in front of it). All other parts of your property are clearly off limits to buyers. The yard sale is another good example. All merchandise is out in the yard. Customers have nowhere else to go.

If you live in a house and plan to hold your sale in your garage or yard, you have no problem. But if you're going to hold it in your apartment, in your basement, or on your porch, patio, or what-have-you, you may have to create barriers between your sale and nonsale areas. Otherwise, customers may invade nonsale areas and rummage through your personal belongings on the theory that everything is for sale.

These artificial barriers will depend on the layout of your home. You may want to close doors, move furniture around, or hang curtains. Often all that's needed is to post signs that make clear the limits of the sale area.

For a sale held indoors, you should try to locate the sale area as close as possible to the door through which people will be entering and leaving. This makes it easier to keep customers in the sale area. It also helps protect your floor. If it rains or snows on the day of your sale, assume the worst. Some people will be thoughtful and remove wet or muddy overshoes before stepping inside, but others will not. By putting your sale area close to exterior doors, you may save a lot of wear on your floor.

What Time of Year Will You Hold It?

My wife and I once held a two-day sale in January. (We live in Illinois.) On the eve of our sale a mass of Arctic air moved in, dropping the temperature to −20 degrees Fahrenheit. All of fourteen customers showed up on the first day, and nobody came on the second day.

Extremely hot weather won't stop many people from coming to your sale, but very cold weather will. So will snow, ice, and heavy rain. If at all possible, avoid holding your sale at times of the year when the probability of any of these things happening is greatest.

In most parts of the United States, the best garage sale weather comes between mid-spring and mid-fall. Those of you who live in a temperate climate can do especially well with a sale held in early spring, if you are lucky enough to schedule it when the weather is pleasant. In the weeks after a long, snowbound winter, the people who patronize these sales flock to them with more than the usual enthusiasm.

What Day or Days Will You Hold It?

The days you hold your sale may be determined by your job, your family responsibilities, or some other factors. If you have a choice, here are some points to consider:

The length of your sale. The longer your sale lasts, the less you'll probably sell on each sale day. If you have a lot of time and want to keep your sale going until everything is sold, then by all means schedule a sale running for a week or more. Otherwise you may be better off limiting your sale to one, two, or three days, depending on how much time you can or are willing to devote to the venture.

Weekends. Sale days near or on the weekend are better than days early in the week. Thursdays, Fridays, and Saturdays are the traditional "garage sale" days in many areas, and sellers who work full-time often hold their sales on Saturdays and Sundays. (However, unless you're in a resort area during "the season" or live on or near a heavily traveled highway or street, Sunday business is sometimes very slow.) Most garage sale buffs do their "junking" on or near weekends. Also, paydays usually fall at the end of the week, putting cash in the hands of your potential buyers. If you plan to sell many tools or other items traditionally used by men, your sale should extend at least into Saturday. Many men like to go to these sales but are unable to do so except on weekends—and this holds equally true for working women.

Newspaper publication dates. The publication dates of the newspapers carrying your ads could be a factor in determining your sale days. The best starting day for your sale would be the day after the newspaper comes out. This would give all interested readers, even those who get their paper late in the day, time to plan to be at your sale the next morning.

What Time of Day Should You Hold It?

Your sale hours may also be determined by circumstances beyond your control. The best time is from 9:00 or 9:30 a.m. until whatever hour you wish to finish. Starting times are more important than finishing times.

No matter what starting time you select, some people will probably show up early. If you complete most of your preparations the night before and set a 9:00 a.m. starting time, you'll be ready as soon as most of your customers are. If you set a starting time for noon or later, planning to complete your last-minute preparations on the morning of the sale, people will show up all morning anyhow. They'll interrupt you long before you're ready for them.

Of course, you can refuse to allow anyone in until your midday starting time. But bear in mind that many garage sale regulars plan their "junking" trips on the basis of their lists of every sale beginning that day, no matter what the announced starting time. If you turn all of these early arrivals away—and some of them are potentially your best customers—you may lose their business altogether.

What Will You Try to Sell?

This question is not as simple as it seems. In deciding what to sell at your garage sale, you should keep an open mind. The type and variety of the goods you have to sell will be a big factor in determining whether your sale will be a success. Generally speaking, these are the factors you should consider:

Quantity of merchandise. The more goods you offer for sale, the more you are likely to sell. A large merchandise display encourages people to stick around longer, looking everything over carefully to be sure they don't miss anything. The longer they linger, the greater chance they'll find something to buy.

Desirability of merchandise. No matter how useless an item might seem to you, someone may want it. Anything might sell. The rotting lumber under your porch, the rusting bicycle wheel in your garage, the no-longer-working radio or stereo gathering dust in the closet—haul all those things out for your sale and put a price on them, no matter how minimal.

If the radio or stereo, the rusted bicycle, or an electrical appliance isn't in working condition, put a "DOES NOT WORK" sign on it. If the price is low enough, someone may buy it just for the challenge of getting it to work. Others may buy it for spare parts.

Emphasis on low prices. Your main concern in holding a sale may be to dispose of some expensive appliances or furniture, but even this will be easier if you have plenty of low-priced merchandise too. The more low-price items you have, the more people will buy. Sales generate more sales. The "buying spirit" is infectious. People seeing other people walking out with armloads of merchandise will get in the spirit and begin buying too.

Another reason for having a lot of low-price items is that many of the people who go to these sales are operating on a shoestring budget. They have only so much to spend. If most of your merchandise is in a medium- or high-price bracket, you will price most of these people out of your market. With a good selection of lower-price items, you're giving all your customers as many chances to buy as possible.

Children's toys. Even if you don't have children of your own, offer a few simple, durable old dolls or other toys that you've picked up inexpensively at rummage sales or other garage sales while doing your market research. While the children play with these, their parents will have more time to look around at the things you really want to sell.

6

You'll Need Help—
But How Much?

The more things you can find to sell, the more work you'll have to do to make the sale a success. You'll want all the help you can get, both from the point of view of making the sale go smoothly and for reasons of security. (For more details on security, see Chapter 12.)

If you're part of a family living together, enlist as many family members as you can for the project. If you're living alone, consider asking a friend, neighbor, or relative to give you a hand "minding the store" while the sale is going on, at least during the first few hours.

The Joint Sale: Pros and Cons

One way to get help for your sale would be to let others in on it. There are many pros and cons about the joint sale, in which two or more sellers pool their efforts. The joint sale spreads the work load and gives buyers a bigger selection of merchandise. It's especially practical for neighboring housewives or for families who share many social activities anyhow. Often the communal garage sale becomes a semi-social event that combines business with pleasure.

But before organizing or agreeing to take part in a joint sale, be sure you can get along with the other member or members of the selling group. Many decisions will have to be made and many problems will arise. If members of the group are not compatible, there'll be squabbling and bad feelings when disagreements arise. The resulting hostility will affect the efficiency with which the sale is run. And in addition to costing you money, these personality clashes could also mean the end of some long-standing friendships.

The main disadvantage of the joint sale is that you are no longer in control. Others may be making decisions for you. If this makes you uncomfortable, by all means avoid the joint sale.

Types of Joint Sales

If you decide on a joint sale and can get people to agree to go in on one with you, your next decision is what type of joint sale it will be.

Usually, in a joint sale all merchandise is hauled to the house or apartment of one member of the group and sold there. This requires setting up a record-keeping system to assure that purchases are credited to the right sellers. Many groups do this by coding price tags to identify each seller. Each item is listed as it is sold. If the tags are removable, they can also be pulled from items and pasted to a "sold" sheet for tabulation later (see Appendix B).

Whatever the mechanics of your system, accounts are settled at the end of each day or when the sale is over.

There are also joint sales in which each member of the group has his or her own selling space in the selling area. In effect, this is a small-scale flea market with each seller responsible for his own merchandise.

This eliminates a lot of record keeping, but all members of the selling group must be present nearly all the time. It may also confuse and discourage buyers. People who go to house and garage sales are accustomed to wandering around, picking up items and paying one person for everything as they leave.

Whatever system you use, all members of the group must understand it before the sale begins. Responsibilities during the sale should be clearly designated. If the selling group is large, it might be a good idea to elect a sale chairman. That person would have final authority to settle disputes and make key decisions.

In a variation of the joint sale where sellers have adjoining or nearby homes or apartments, each group member displays and sells on his or her own property. The sale's "joint" aspects are mainly agreeing on sale dates and pooling funds and efforts in a cooperative advertising program.

Larger sales of this type can be very successful. Whole blocks and even neighborhoods have cooperated in staging them. By stressing the large number of sellers, the advertising and publicity can draw buyers from much greater distances than you could expect otherwise. Sellers sell from garages, yards, porches, basements, or wherever is most convenient.

If these big community sales are held every year, they will build a following of buyers as time goes on. Of course when sales are this big, it's essential to have a chairperson or committee to coordinate activities and be responsible for advertising and publicity. Chapter 14 on "Fund-Raising Garage Sales" may be helpful if you're thinking of organizing a sale of this magnitude.

Should You Take Items on Consignment?

You can assemble a greater variety of items to sell by taking some goods on consignment from your friends, relatives, or neighbors. These items are displayed with yours. If you sell any, you get a commission.

Consignment sales are a mixed blessing. They give you more things to sell and get more people interested in your sale. Rest assured, people who consign items with you will help promote your sale through word-of-mouth. And of course the commissions will add to your profits.

On the other hand, you may not want to be responsible for other people's merchandise, or to bother with the record keeping that may be required. Consignment selling can also result in misunderstandings and disputes, ruining beautiful friendships. There's also the chance some consignors will abuse the privilege, loading you with too many items or items you'd rather not handle.

Rules for Consignment Sellers

If you decide to take items on consignment, these are the essential points to take into consideration:

Waiver of responsibility. Have it clearly understood that you won't be responsible if items are damaged or stolen. If you are dealing with people who are not close friends of yours, or if the items are especially valuable, it might be wise to have this understanding formalized in writing.

A system to credit consignment sales accurately. As with joint sales, you could code price tags to identify sellers and list items as they are sold. Or if you are using removable tags, they could be pulled from the items when sold and pasted to a sheet for later tabulation.

Another way would be to assign each consignor a code letter, then require him or her to tag their own items with prices and their code letter and to give you a list of them. When a consigned item is sold, all you do is make a notation or checkmark on the consignor's list. (See Appendix B for examples of all three methods.)

A required minimum price. Why get bogged down with a lot of record keeping over nickel-and-dime items that don't even belong to you? Consider requiring that consignors bring nothing but better merchandise costing at least $1 or $5.

Accurate records of payments to consignors. If you make payments to a consignor during the sale, keep a record of that too. In the confusion of a sale, it's easier to forget these things than you might think.

Control over your merchandise. Don't be afraid to exercise control over what your consignors want you to sell. It is possible that one or more consignors will put prices on their items that you know are far too high. If they do, for your own protection, insist that they lower their prices to more realistic levels. People who attend your sale will assume everything is yours. If they see even a single item priced far more than they know it's worth, they'll categorize you as a price gouger.

It's also possible that, for reasons of taste or personal preference, you'll want to control the type of items offered by your consignors.

Since it is your sale, insist on any criteria you wish. Similarly, don't hesitate to call a halt if a consignor brings more items than you want to handle.

How Much Commission Should You Charge?

The phrase "ten-percenter" has been popularized in novels and dramas involving theatrical or literary agents. Probably that's why many people holding garage sales charge only 10 percent commission when they take consignments. In my opinion, under normal circumstances that's not enough. Usually the consignor does nothing but list and tag merchandise and then bring it to the sale. The person holding the sale pays for the advertising, makes and sets out signs and other promotional materials, and minds the store during the sale.

Entertainers and authors have invested years of time and effort in developing their talents or writing their books. They are entitled to most of the fruits of their labor. But the only things your consignors contribute are used household goods.

At the other end of the scale, resale and consignment shops often demand one-third or even one-half of the selling price of what you bring in. However, the shop owners must rent a store, get a license, take out insurance, and meet all their other business expenses, including salaries. They also devote their year-round time to the business, and have developed contacts with antique dealers, collectors, and other big buyers who visit their shops regularly, assuring a market.

The one-third to one-half cut is justified by the contributions professional shop owners make, but it may be too high for people running garage sales. Generally speaking, a commission rate of 20 or 25 percent for handling consignment items at these sales seems fair.

This should be modified by circumstances, however. You probably wouldn't charge a commission if your consignors helped you run the sale. Taking things on consignment could also be a way to repay a friend or neighbor for past favors. And of course if the consignor is an old or dear friend, you may not want to charge a commission under any circumstances.

7

How to Advertise Your Sale

While we were gathering material for this book, my wife and I talked to many people who hold garage sales on the spur of the moment and do very well. If the weather's nice and they have no other weekend plans, they quickly assemble and tag some merchandise, put up a few signs announcing the sale, and sit back to await buyers.

If you enjoy holding these sales, this can be a profitable and pleasant activity for one family, couple, or single person, or for several working together. From an economic standpoint, it certainly beats a weekend in which you spend money for entertainment rather than making money while entertaining yourself. To be at all successful, however, a sale held on this extemporaneous basis must be on or near a high-traffic street or highway. And whatever the sale's results, it would have been far more successful if you had promoted it properly.

The greater the number of people who hear about your sale, the more potential buyers you'll attract. The spur-of-the-moment sale is fine if you understand its limitations. But for maximum returns from a garage sale, you must plan and carry out a well-rounded advertising campaign.

Use Free Advertising

Many supermarkets and other stores have bulletin boards on which, for no charge, you can post advance notices of your sale. Don't limit yourself to the stores in your immediate neighborhood. Spend some time putting notices on all the bulletin boards within a reasonable driving range of your sale. In addition, some local merchants may allow you to post signs in their windows. If you or someone in your family works where there is a company bulletin board, see about posting a notice there. Similarly, you may be able to post notices on the bulletin boards of religious or civic organizations to which you belong.

The Importance of "Word-of-Mouth" Advertising

The most effective free advertising is "word-of-mouth" advertising spread by people who know you. Tell your friends, relatives, neighbors, and co-workers about your sale. They'll be potential customers themselves and will pass the word to *their* friends, relatives, and neighbors—especially if they know someone who might be in the market for some of the more expensive items you may want to sell.

Advertise in Local Newspapers

Newspapers are the most important part of your advertising and promotion campaign. It would be a big mistake to try to reduce your expenses by eliminating newspaper advertising. This would pay only if you had very little to sell, or lived in a community so small and isolated that nearly all of your potential buyers would learn about your sale through signs or word of mouth.

Newspaper advertising is usually essential because this is how most hard-core garage and house sale buffs learn about sales. They closely follow the classified columns in their daily, weekly, or community papers. Many use the ads to map out their garage sale "routes" for the day.

On the other hand, when planning your advertising campaign, don't spend more money than necessary. If many papers serve your community, concentrate on the one(s) that will do you the most good. You can get advice on this from other sellers when you do your market research. As a rule, the most effective papers will be the ones with the greatest number of "Garage Sale" ads.

Also, be sure to time your advertising carefully. Learn the advertising deadlines of your newspapers. If you're advertising in a daily paper, your ad(s) should not appear until a day or two before the sale. If it's a weekly paper, run the ad in the issue published on or just before the day the sale is to start.

There are two good reasons for not advertising too far in advance. First, most garage sale customers are interested only in sales they can go to "right now." Second, early advertising may bring you an unusual number of "early birds" who will interrupt your last-minute preparations by trying to see what you have to sell ahead of time.

What to Say in Your Ads

The size of your ads should be determined by how much you have to sell. If you have just a few things and they're of no great value, get small ads. But if you have a big selection, including some expensive items, it will pay to run big ads. For maximum results you should take ads big enough to list all the categories of what you have to sell—books, clothing, tools, tires, toys, etc.—as well as some of the more important individual items.

There's no doubt that the bigger your ads and the more merchandise you describe, the more buyers you'll attract. It's just a matter of deciding at what point the higher costs will outweigh the additional revenue brought in by the bigger ads.

Whatever the size of your ads, a few well-chosen words or phrases, such as "much miscellaneous" or "loads of junque," can suggest a great diversity of merchandise. And instead of just announcing "Garage Sale," call it a "Mammoth Garage Sale," "Giant Garage Sale," or what-have-you. Don't try to get fancy or cute. Stick to the facts.

If yours is a communal sale, make that clear too: "Huge Three-Family Garage Sale," etc. The more merchandise people think you have, the more they're likely to attend your sale.

If your sale's location would be hard for strangers to find, your ads should mention a landmark pinpointing the location or should include directions on how to get there.

Some sellers list their phone numbers along with their address, but this could be a mistake. When the sale starts, you'll be busy enough taking money, wrapping merchandise, negotiating, answering questions, and otherwise minding the store. A constantly ringing phone with calls from people who may have many questions to ask would be a serious distraction. Another reason for not including your phone number is that many callers will inquire only about a specific item or category of items. If you don't have these items, they won't come to your sale. But if they don't have your phone number, they might come, see something else that interests them, and buy that.

There are also sellers who omit their address and just put their phone numbers in their ads. In this way you can screen out callers who seem undesirable to you, but you'll also screen out most of your potential market. Many people are too timid to phone, and others just won't bother.

Outdoor Advertising

Good outdoor signs are also very important. You should start planning and making them well in advance of your sale. During the sale you will need a sign in front of your home where it can easily be seen by passing motorists. If you live on a quiet side street, the sign needn't be large. But if you live on a street where motorists may be driving at a fast pace, it should be big enough to be read easily from a distance. Otherwise, drivers may miss it or see it so late that they can't stop safely.

One reason for the outdoor sign is to help people who have heard about your sale through newspaper or other advertising find your home. It's part of your overall strategy of making it as easy as possible for people to buy.

But another reason is that the sign itself will draw customers.

Signs Attract People

The degree to which outdoor signs alone will lure buyers is not fully appreciated by many people holding a sale for the first time. Never underestimate the pulling power of a well-placed sign proclaiming "GARAGE SALE," "ESTATE SALE," "BASEMENT SALE," "PORCH SALE," or even simply "SALE." Every bargain hunter, collector, or junque addict who drives by and has a moment to spare will stop to see what you have to offer. It's a compulsion they can't resist.

In fact, the longer your sale goes on, the more important your signs become. After two days of a three-day sale, most of the people who have seen your newspaper or bulletin board ads will have been there. A larger and larger proportion of your buyers will be casual passers-by attracted solely by your sign.

Some sellers go to elaborate lengths with their outdoor advertising. They construct huge sandwich-board signs for the front of their houses or decorate the site with ribbons and balloons, just as builders do when displaying model homes. This is sound merchandising; it imparts a touch of the carnival atmosphere that buyers seem to enjoy. But if you don't have the time or inclination for these ornate touches, any easy-to-read outdoor sign announcing your sale will do the job.

Help Buyers Find You

You should place signs along arterial streets and highways and at major intersections within a reasonable distance of your sale. These signs should announce the sale, give the address, and perhaps include an arrow pointing in the direction motorists should go. The best locations for these signs are major intersections where drivers slowing down for a stop sign or traffic light will have time to see and read them.

Many newspapers give garage sale signs to people buying garage sale ads. Some Realtors give signs to people who buy or sell a home through them, and some variety stores sell printed signs.

If you are making your own signs, do the lettering as legibly as you can, and be sure the letters are big enough to be read from a moving car. Use indelible markers if there is any chance of rain or snow. Otherwise a storm may wash them out or make them unreadable. (But in marking your merchandise, do *not* use indelible markers: See Chapter 9, "Last-Minute Preparations.")

8

All About Pricing

The most important preparation for your garage sale will be to put price tags on everything you hope to sell. Yes, it takes time to price and tag everything. But you have much to lose and nothing to gain by not doing so.

Some sellers fail to price and tag their merchandise because they're lazy. Others intend to make price tags but don't allow enough time. Still others don't tag items because of an odd notion that they may get higher prices by forcing buyers to make the first offer.

Nonsense! For each "better" deal you may get that way, you'll lose dozens of sales you could have made if your prices were marked.

Why Everything Should Be Priced

The reasons for pricing everything are:

To make it easier for people to buy. All your preparations should be aimed at making buying as easy as possible. You can't expect people to seek you out to ask "How much is this?" each time they see an item that interests them. Look at it this way: How much time would *you* spend in a store—and your sale *is* a "store"—if you had to find a clerk to ask the price of everything on display? Assuming that the clerk wasn't too busy to talk to you because he or she was quoting prices to someone else? Unless you had a compelling interest in the item, you'd leave and go to a store where prices were marked. And so will many of the people who come to your sale.

To identify bargains. Many of the people who regularly visit house and garage sales have nothing specific in mind. They're simply hoping to find bargains, and they will buy practically anything if they think the price is right. The only way to let them know that an item they didn't dream they wanted is a bargain is to put a price tag on it.

To encourage buyers. Many people are timid about asking prices. They don't want to haggle. If they don't see a price on an item, they'll assume that the only way they can buy it is by haggling. Other people may assume that the absence of price tags means you're trying to put something over on them.

To protect yourself. Nobody can remember everything, especially if it's your first sale and you're confused by a lot of things suddenly happening all at once. If you must quote prices off the top of your head, you'll risk making mistakes. If you quote too high a price, you'll kill the sale; if your price is too low, you won't get as much as you should.

To make the sale go smoothly. If you've tagged all your merchandise, you won't have to spend time answering questions about how much this or that costs. You can concentrate on the more positive aspects of selling, such as pleasantly greeting just-arrived customers, stressing an item's strong points, and completing sales.

How Much Should It Cost?

It would be impossible for me or anyone else to give meaningful advice on what to charge for merchandise at a house or garage sale. An almost infinite variety of merchandise is offered at these sales, ranging from used clothing and the most commonplace household goods to the whole spectrum of collectibles and antiques. An even partially comprehensive pricing guide would require thousands of pages.

The value of any used item is affected by its condition. People in the trade sometimes observe that "you can't put a price on an antique." This is also true of used household goods. Each item is unique. Over the years, it has acquired its own nicks, dents, scratches, scars, stains, or other signs of wear and is now unlike any other item anywhere.

Further, there are regional variations in price levels. Generally speaking, antique prices are lower on the East Coast than in the West. Most antiques of American origin come from the East because most of the West was sparsely populated until late in the 19th century.

In addition, prices may fluctuate for seasonal and other reasons. If you live where snow falls in winter, you'll get a better price for used snow tires in December than in May. And when collectors decide to begin accumulating heretofore ignored items, prices can rise rapidly. (Of course when items fall out of favor with collectors, prices can also drop rapidly!)

Again, this is why it can pay to visit other garage sales, rummage sales, flea markets, resale shops, and antique shops and shows before holding your own sale. Knowing what you have to sell, you can see the range of prices for comparable merchandise. The closer you can price your items to the lower end of this range, the easier it will be to sell them.

You Can't Ask Store Prices in a Garage

Many first-time sellers underprice their merchandise. Usually this is because they are ignorant of its market value. This is especially true of elderly people, who often don't realize that some of the "everyday" things accumulated in their younger years are now desired by collectors.

But a more common mistake made by inexperienced sellers is to set prices too high.

There's a saying to the effect that a little knowledge is a dangerous thing. For many people, this is all too true when they set prices at their garage sale. They've seen an item priced at a certain level at a resale store or antique shop, and they assume that a similar item they are selling is "worth" that too.

But it isn't. When you're establishing prices for a house or garage sale, you're not competing with retail stores and antique shops, you're competing with the people running other house and garage sales.

To put it another way: People won't pay store prices for things they buy from strangers in basements and garages.

You're in a Wholesale Market

When you buy from a store, the store's name and reputation stand behind your purchase. Be it a seller of new merchandise or an antique shop, the store usually offers some or all of the following: return privileges, check cashing, consumer credit, a guarantee or warranty, and many other services.

This means that to be truly competitive, your prices must be substantially below store prices. As noted earlier, garage sales are part of a wholesale market that supplies retail antique and junque shops. Indeed, although they may not identify themselves, some of your customers will almost certainly be the owners of antique and resale stores.

It's true that you can violate pricing rules and make some sales at high prices to uninformed buyers, but your total sales volume will be less than if you price your merchandise realistically. Don't kid yourself. The people who go to these sales include some of the shrewdest shoppers in your town. That's why they're poking around in your garage instead of browsing in stores.

You Can't Win Them All

Setting prices for a garage sale is at best an inexact science. Your general strategy will depend on your reasons for holding the sale. If it's to clean out your attic or dispose of as much stuff as possible before moving, you'll price lower than if you hope to "get your money back" or show a profit.

In any event, when setting prices you're bound to make mistakes. You can't know the value of everything. Even after doing your market research, you'll price some items too high and others too low, so don't spend too much time trying to determine the "best" price for every item. Antique and resale shop dealers make pricing mistakes too. Just go through what you have and set prices you think are reasonable.

After your sale starts, you can justifiably suspect that many of the items snatched up in the first hour were probably priced too low. And after it ends, you can conclude that much of the merchandise still unsold was priced too high.

Here are two good general pricing rules to keep in mind:

> Try to set your prices lower than people would pay for comparable items at a store, but higher than what you'd get from a dealer.

> Try to set the highest price at which people still can't resist buying the item even if they don't need it.

General Pricing Tips

No book can tell you exactly what price to charge for anything, but here is some general advice based on the experiences of people who have held many sales.

These sales are great for disposing of wedding, Christmas, or other gifts that you can't use or don't want (provided the people who gave you the gifts don't come to the sale). But even if what you want to sell is new and in the original package, don't expect to get anything like the typical store price. Realistically, unless there's something very special about what you're trying to sell, you may be lucky to get half of the store price.

Shoes, used clothing (unless of very high quality), curtains, and old purses bring very little money and should be priced accordingly. Small used appliances are hard to sell except at rock-bottom prices, and most magazines are of little value unless they are very old or "collectible"—which mainly means major magazines no longer being published or of ancient vintage. However, *Playboy, Oui, Penthouse,* and other major men's magazines are always salable, and of these *Playboy* is the most collectible.

To clean out paperback books, don't charge more than a nickel or a dime apiece. Unless there is something especially valuable about a hardcover book, don't charge more than a quarter, or a half-dollar if it's in especially good condition. In most cases your old college textbooks are virtually worthless. Old typewriters in working condition usually sell if priced at $15 or less.

There is always a strong demand for small tables and bookcases and for other small pieces of furniture if they are priced right (which means low). Upholstered furniture is sometimes harder to sell because it is bulky and may not fit in with anyone's décor. Also, rips and tears can kill a sale.

Original artwork in a wood frame should command a high price. It's easier to sell prints if you put them in frames that are in good condition. "By-the-numbers" paintings are of no value except to the artist, but reasonably priced picture frames are always good sellers. And there is always a strong market for reasonably priced figurines, paperweights, other small knickknacks, clay flowerpots, and toys and games in good condition.

Other top sellers, if priced reasonably, are pots and pans in good condition, other kitchen items, costume jewelry, full or nearly full bottles of cologne or other toiletries, tools, linens, and towels. Drapes are hard to sell because of size problems, and if cake or pie pans are rusty, nobody is likely to buy them at any price.

To Bargain or Not to Bargain?

Some of the people who come to your sale will offer to buy items for less than the prices on your tags. To them, haggling is part of the game. No matter how low your price is to begin with, they'll try to buy the item for less. How you handle these people depends on many things, including your ability and willingness to engage in bargaining sessions.

If you'd rather not haggle, then set a "firm price" policy and stick to it. If your prices are reasonable, it's not a bad idea, either. Most people who make offers won't be offended if you turn them down in a polite way. If your price is fair and they want the item, they'll probably buy it anyhow.

The safest policy if you *are* willing to haggle would be to tag items a little over your "rock-bottom" price. Of course you'll have more pricing leeway on some items than others. Decide before the sale starts how far you'll be willing to lower prices in a bargaining session.

If you want to be a real gambler, price all of your merchandise substantially above what you view as your "rock bottom" and then be prepared to haggle over everything. But to do this, you must also be a thick-skinned extrovert. This tactic will also cut you off from buyers who don't want to haggle, and it will risk alienating people who will decide you are a price gouger.

Keep an Open Mind

Even if you don't want to bargain, the prices on your tags should not be inflexible. There are a number of circumstances under which you should be willing to lower prices during your sale.

For example, after the sale has been going on for a while, you may well decide it would be better to sell something far below your tag price than to be stuck with it unsold.

If someone offers to buy a large number of items and asks for a price concession on the basis of the volume purchase, you should probably give the buyer a break. He is absorbing in one transaction some items that you very possibly would not otherwise sell. It would be wise to avoid any volume purchase discounts in the early hours of your sale. But the longer your sale goes on, the better these deals will be for you.

9

Last-Minute Preparations

Much of your time on the day or so before the sale will be spent setting prices, tagging merchandise, and arranging your merchandise displays. The more merchandise you have, the more time you should allow. The job should be virtually completed before your sale starts.

What Kind of Tags?

Many people selling secondhand goods, some dealers included, use ordinary masking tape to make their price tags. This is the cheapest tagging system. You cut off a piece of tape, affix it to the item, and mark the price on the tape. But masking tape has many drawbacks. It's a slow tagging method. If you have several hundred items to tag,

50

t takes a lot of extra time to pull tape off the roll and hand-cut each tag. What's more, not all writing instruments mark effectively on masking tape's rough, somewhat absorbent surface. It's also the sloppiest-looking way to tag merchandise—and if you're using an indelible marker, there are circumstances under which marker fluid can penetrate the tape and damage the item. The glue on the tape itself can also cause damage.

Under no circumstances should you use conventional gummed mailing labels. They are very difficult to remove and can permanently damage some surfaces.

With some marking instruments, prices can be marked directly onto glass, metal, porcelain, pottery, and other hard, washable surfaces. But if you do this, be sure you are not using an indelible marker. The marks must be easy to wipe or wash off.

Never put *any* mark directly on an item until you've experimented and are *sure* the mark can be removed. To be on the safe side, don't mark any item directly unless it's a low-price item.

One relatively satisfactory way to mark items is with paper fastened by transparent tape. While cumbersome, this is inexpensive and fairly safe.

If you're willing to spend a dollar or two, you might invest in some pressure-sensitive adhesive tags. The more items you must tag, the more this investment pays for itself in time and convenience. These tags are easy to apply and relatively easy to remove. Your customers will appreciate that, and so will you. As your sale progresses, you may decide to change some prices. Switching tags is easier and quicker with these tags than with other marking systems. And when the sale is over, it'll be easy to remove these tags from unsold merchandise.

No matter what system you use, be careful. Don't put tags or marks where they can't be removed easily without risking damage to the item.

Clean Up Your Merchandise

One thing almost uniformly stressed by people who have held successful garage sales is the importance of making your merchandise as attractive and serviceable as you reasonably can.

Items that are clean and in good shape will get higher prices than like items covered with dust or in disrepair.

Don't knock yourself out trying to polish every rusty old garden implement. But dishes, glassware, and crockery should be washed; clothing and linens should be cleaned; furniture and pictures should be dusted; and silver should be polished.

You should also make any simple, obvious repairs. It won't pay to get bogged down in major fix-up jobs, but it only takes a minute to drive a nail or apply a dab of paint or glue.

Point-of-Sale Signs

Your last-minute preparations will include completing the signs for outside your house or apartment, as well as other signs to be posted along the streets. This is covered in Chapter 7, "How to Advertise Your Sale."

You may also need some point-of-sale signs. For instance, if your merchandise is to be displayed in two or more locations on your property, signs should announce that. You may decide to put some merchandise outside in your yard or patio, with the remainder in the basement or on a porch. A sign in the yard should indicate that there is more to see, with an arrow pointing the way.

If your sale is in your basement, porch, or some other part of your home, put up a sign indicating the door through which you want people to enter. If it's not necessary for people to ring or knock, put a "PLEASE WALK IN" sign on the door. (And when your sale ends, don't forget to take *that* sign down immediately.)

Other signs you may want in your sale area include:

Information about merchandise not in the sale area. Some furniture may be too heavy to move there. Other items may be so fragile or valuable that you don't want them handled casually by curiosity-seekers or children.

More information about items you're selling. If a piece is especially old or has some novel or unique aspect, a sign should point that out.

"NOT FOR SALE" signs. Affix these to anything in the sale area you don't want to sell and would rather not have examined, handled, and possibly damaged.

Some sellers also put up signs inviting people to leave bids on their most expensive items. If these items are not sold by the end of the sale, they go to the highest bidder.

Be Ready to Make Change

Making change will become less of a problem after your sale runs for a while. But if you're not able to make change during the opening hours, you could inconvenience your customers. This could even cost you a sale or two, and in any event it will distract you from more important tasks. If you anticipate a fair volume of business, go to the bank a day or so before your sale and get a roll each of nickels ($2 worth), dimes ($5 worth), and quarters ($10). Also get twenty $1 bills, a few $5 bills, and at least one or two $10 bills.

Know What You'll Do with Your Money

You'll need a plan for handling the money you take in. It's not likely that anyone will come to your sale planning to steal it, but there's no point in being so careless that you'll risk being victimized. Currency will be safer on your person than in a cigar box, purse, or other container that may, for one reason or another, be left unattended, no matter how briefly.

One solution is to keep most of your currency in a money clip. The advantage of a money clip is that you can keep it in a pocket where it is easy to reach, and you won't have to expose a bulky wallet that may also contain credit cards and valuable papers.

If your sale goes well, currency may stack up quickly. It is prudent to take out some bills periodically and secrete them in a secure part of your home rather than displaying too big a pile in front of strangers. You'll also accumulate a lot of change. Coins are too heavy to store in a pocket, unless you have a carpenter's apron. Put them in a box or other container, and have a system for keeping the box under observation and control at all times.

Have a Credit Policy

Anyone selling merchandise to the public must have a credit policy, and garage sales are no exception. Sooner or later, someone will ask if you'll take a personal check.

If you feel uncomfortable at the idea of accepting a check instead of cash, you should plan ahead what you'll say and how you'll say it. You don't want to offend a customer with a hasty, unintentionally rude remark. It would be best to explain cordially that there's nothing personal in your decision, but you're simply not prepared to handle checks; you're terribly sorry, but you can only conduct business on a cash-and-carry basis.

If you have firmly decided on this policy, place a sign prominently in your sale area stating: "ALL SALES CASH, PLEASE," or "NO CHECKS, PLEASE."

There's always some risk in accepting checks from strangers. On the other hand, if you don't accept checks you could miss some big sales. Many people simply don't carry much cash with them. They're accustomed to paying with checks or credit cards, and they may be offended no matter how politely you turn them down.

One way to handle the would-be buyer who doesn't have enough cash is to accept a deposit and hold the item until he or she returns with full payment.

Set Up Your "Command Headquarters"

In arranging your sale area, make a place for yourself. It should have a table or other flat working space, plus chairs for you and anyone helping you. The location of your "command headquarters" will depend on the layout of your sale area. If possible, put it where you can greet people as they arrive and check them out as they leave. Your headquarters should be equipped with:

Marking and tagging equipment. You will need this for replacing lost or damaged tags or making tags with new prices.

Sign-making equipment. You may end up making signs the need for which is not apparent until the sale gets under way. For instance, so many people may wander into nonsale areas that you'll decide you need some "PLEASE KEEP OUT" signs.

Pencil and paper. You will need these for making computations when people buy more than one item. But if you own or can borrow a small adding machine, by all means use it. It will save time and reduce errors. Printing machines are best, because you can quickly double-check your calculations—some people may buy many items—and then give buyers the tape as a receipt.

Record-keeping equipment. This will enable you to log sales of consigned items or to credit items sold at joint sales.

Help Them Carry It Away

In line with your policy of making it easy for people to buy, you should provide bags to help them carry the merchandise away. For a month or so before the sale, put aside all the bags you bring home from shopping trips. Haul them out for your sale and store them at your "command headquarters."

Your wrapping department should also include newspapers, for wrapping glassware and other fragile items, and some sizable boxes for people who buy a lot of merchandise.

Don't Make It Look Too Much Like a Store

The merchandise display at your garage sale should be attractive, but don't go overboard. Being neat and tidy is one thing. Dressing up your sale area to where it begins to resemble a store is something else. At some so-called garage and basement sales, merchandise is so professionally laid out in display cases that the atmosphere resembles that of a high-class (and high-price) antique shop. I've even seen garage sales where you check out at a cash register.

This is a mistake. People go to garage sales to find bargains sold by private parties. A too-professional atmosphere intimidates some buyers. In fact, if your sale area begins to look too much like a store, you might try hoking it up with some "bargain boxes" and a general air of homey disarray.

Displaying Your Merchandise

Here are some tips on displaying merchandise:

Put like items together. This will make it easier for collectors and other people interested in that general type of merchandise to find it.

Use sturdy "counters." Tables, benches, and other objects holding merchandise must be strong enough to remain standing even though jostled, which they almost inevitably will be.

Try to prevent breakage. When arranging items on a counter or table, put the small items in front and the big ones in back. This will lessen the chances of items in front being knocked down when someone reaches out for an item in the back. And keep breakable items away from table, counter, or shelf edges. If you have a "quarter box," "penny box," or other box filled with merchandise jumbled together, be sure the merchandise can take a lot of punishment. People will treat it roughly.

Allow elbowroom. Is there enough room in the aisles for people to move without bumping into one another? Or into your display tables? Are the aisles clear? Lamps or other electrical appliances with cords in or near an aisle are especially big hazards. After your first customer stumbles over a cord, perhaps taking a lamp and/or table down too, you won't make that mistake again.

Provide electric outlets as needed. If you're selling lamps or small appliances, have an outlet available so customers can test them.

Display clothing items effectively. If possible, hang coats, dresses, jackets, sweaters, etc., on a rack or clothesline rather than piling them in a heap on a table. Buyers can see the clothing more easily, and it will take less of a beating. Also, if you're selling hats, outerwear, or other clothing that people might try on, have a mirror available.

Keep your merchandise accessible. It's all right to put merchandise on the floor or under the tables, but don't block your tables. Buyers must be able to reach everything on the table.

Create a "gallery" for pictures. If you're selling many pictures, hang them up, or spread them out by leaning them against a wall, fence, furniture, etc. People buy pictures on impulse. They don't even know they want a picture until they see the right one. Also, pictures piled in a box will be damaged by people rummaging through the box.

Be aware of traffic flow. If possible, display books where people can browse without blocking aisles. Also, try to put toys off by themselves so traffic patterns won't be clogged by children playing with them.

Make sure typewriters, etc., are functional. Typewriters, adding machines, and printing calculators should be in working condition. If necessary, invest in a new ribbon. Hardly anyone will buy these machines without trying them. Put paper in typewriters and display them on surfaces sturdy enough for someone to test them.

Hold back merchandise if necessary. If your space is limited and you have many specialized collector's items of the same kind, put only some out. Leave the others near the display area where they'll be seen and can be examined, or make a small sign saying more are available. Be sure they're where you can get them easily if someone wants to see them.

Label tires clearly. When selling automobile tires, paste big stickers on them giving their size and, if you know, the cars they'll fit. This will attract buyers who might otherwise overlook them.

Check the lighting in your sale area. On overcast days, the interiors of some garages and basements are dim and gloomy. If your sale area lacks adequate lighting, rig temporary lights so buyers can see what you have to sell. What they can't see, they won't buy.

Keep "special handling" items separate. If you don't want an item handled, don't put it where it can *be* handled. Store it on a high shelf or in a locked case or cabinet.

Special Outdoor Problems

If your display space is outdoors, you may have special problems stemming from weather conditions. Even a moderate gust of wind can knock down tall, fragile items. If it's a windy day, lay those items on their sides rather than standing them up.

If there's the merest threat of rain, you should have a contingency plan. Depending on the nature of your display and its location, be ready to move your merchandise inside or to cover it. Flea market sellers usually carry large plastic drop cloths with them for this purpose.

Sunlight can melt candles and even some glues, if repairs are recent. If you'll be outside most of the time, it could also give you a painful case of sunburn. If you're not accustomed to being exposed to the sun, wear a broadbrim hat and something that covers your arms, no matter how warm the day.

Sales Promotion Devices

Depending on how much you have to sell, where you'll be holding your sale, and how much help you'll have, you may also wish to use one or more of these sales promotion devices:

A box of free items. The items in this box would be of minimal value, but this is an effective device. It suggests that your main reason for holding the sale is to clean out your attic or closets, not to make a profit. Also, people taking items from a "freebie box" usually feel obliged to buy something too. Of course, it won't pay to have a freebie box if you have relatively few things to sell. In that case you'd be better off getting something, no matter how little, for everything you sell.

Free coffee or other refreshments. This is especially effective on raw days. In addition to being a convenience, serving refreshments induces your customers to remain in the sale area. The longer they hang around, the more likely they are to see something to buy. And the longer they linger, the bigger the crowd. The more people congregate, the more they'll fall into the buying spirit.

Of course, you'll need a big sale area to be able to offer coffee or other refreshments, and you'll need other people helping with your sale. You can't be boiling water for coffee while customers with money in their hands are waiting to buy your merchandise.

Background music. Just as in some stores, soft music from a radio or stereo will put people at ease, especially during slack periods when few shoppers are present. It gives people a sense of privacy in talking among themselves that is not possible when "it's so quiet you can hear a pin drop." If you use a radio, tune in a station that plays bland music seldom interrupted by commercials. Avoid stations with jarring music or talk shows that could distract your buyers.

Here Come the "Early Birds"!

The more populous the area in which you live, the more likely that your last-minute preparations for your sale will be interrupted by visits from one or more "early birds." These people aren't content merely to show up early on the day of the sale, a phenomenon you should accept with good humor. No, the "early birds" want more. Usually they've learned of your sale through newspaper ads. Sometimes they have heard of your sale through word of mouth, and occasionally they'll show up even before your ad appears. A few of the more aggressive may even arrange for newspaper employees to tip them off to sale locations before the paper is published.

"Early birds" have all manner of explanations as to why they're there so far in advance. Usually they'll appear the afternoon or evening of the day before your sale is to begin.

What These People Really Want

Some "early birds" will tell you they "won't have the car tomorrow, and can't I please see what you have tonight?" Others will say they're going out of town," or "just happened to be in the neighborhood."

The variety of their cover stories is infinite. To be more convincing, they might claim to be especially interested in a particular type of item, such as "a bookcase for my son, who is a student." But even if you say you have no bookcase, you'll be pressured into showing what you do have. And if you stammer something about how the sale isn't supposed to start until the following day, they'll say very convincingly: "But you want to *sell* your things, don't you? What difference does it make *when* you sell them?"

Whatever they say, you must recognize these "early birds" for what they are. Nearly all of them are semiprofessional dealers or hard-core unque addicts. They're trying to take advantage of your confusion and inexperience to buy something valuable for as close to nothing as possible, and they're hoping your merchandise will include treasures whose true value you fail to recognize. They want to snatch up those bargains before anyone else can. Many also know that in the confusing hours before the sale, you haven't had time to establish all of your prices. You may be rattled by their approach and quote too low a price off the top of your head, or you may accept a ridiculously low offer.

Should You, or Shouldn't You?

All things considered, should you allow these "early birds" into your home, garage, or yard one or more days before the sale, or shouldn't you?

Many people buy the argument that since they want to sell all of their goods anyway, it doesn't matter if they sell some ahead of time. If you're in that camp—and according to interviews with people who have held garage sales, you have plenty of company—just be on guard. You could take a real beating by allowing an "early bird" to prowl through your things before all your prices are set, offering a dollar for this or a quarter for that and wondering "if you couldn't reduce the price a little, it seems so high."

Other people stoutly refuse to allow "early birds" into their homes until the day of the sale. Certainly you should have no qualms of conscience about politely but firmly telling an "early bird" that you're not ready yet and simply don't have time to deal with him or her. If the "early bird" refuses to leave, above all don't be intimidated. Stop being polite and assert your rights. It's your home, and you don't have to tolerate anyone's uninvited presence if you choose not to.

Why I Don't Let "Early Birds" In

Unless they are your friends or neighbors, I'd recommend not allowing any "early birds" into your home until the day of the sale. First of all it isn't fair to customers who do follow the rules. Second, it's more important for you to complete your last-minute preparations—pricing, making signs, cleaning and repairing merchandise, setting up your display area, etc.—than it is to drop everything to show one "early bird" around.

Keep in mind that anything the "early birds" might buy before a sale starts, they will also buy *after* it starts. If you refuse to let them in the day before the sale, almost invariably they'll be first in line the next morning. And unless you have badly underpriced your merchandise, "early birds" don't usually buy much anyhow. If an "early bird" begins buying right and left, your things were worth more than you thought. Let's face it:

Many "early birds" are doing what they do because they want to take advantage of you. Why encourage them?

Finally, all "early birds" are guilty of calculated rudeness. When you place an ad announcing your sale, you are inviting buyers to your home on the sale dates, and those dates only. If you were invited to a friend's house for dinner on Sunday, you wouldn't show up on Saturday and announce: "I'm sorry, but I'm hungry now, so feed me today instead." Yet this is precisely what the "early birds" are doing to you.

For what it's worth, professionals who make a business of holding house, estate, and garage sales for a fee refuse to allow any "early birds" inside ahead of time. In addition to considering them unfair to their other buyers, they know from experience that anything one of them buys would be snatched up in the sale's opening hours anyhow.

Akin to the "early birds" are people who phone before the sale to ask what you have to sell. Even if you don't give your phone number in your ad, you may receive one or more calls from people who got your number by knowing your address. If this happens to you, don't waste much time on the phone. If your caller asks about specific items, respond politely, but don't get yourself in the position of having to start listing virtually everything you're selling. Just say you have so many things that you couldn't possibly describe them all, and invite the caller to come over on the day of the sale to see them with his or her own eyes.

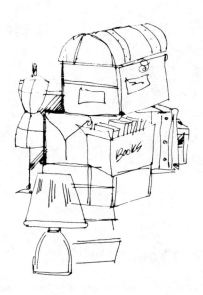

12

Security at Your Sale

It is unlikely that you will have security problems at your garage sale. Most of the sellers interviewed during the preparation of this book reported no security problems whatsoever. However, it would certainly be prudent to anticipate any difficulties that might arise and to take what precautions you can to hold risks to a minimum.

The two potential threats to security are crimes against your property and crimes against your person.

One of the best defenses against both is to have as many people helping with your sale as you can. If possible, at least two people should be present at all times.

Guarding Against Shoplifters

Anyone who sells merchandise to the public risks being victimized by shoplifters. No neighborhoods are immune. In fact, shoplifting problems in wealthy suburbs are often as serious as anywhere else. Well-to-do housewives and children from affluent families may steal for psychological reasons that have nothing to do with the value of the merchandise.

It's not too likely that you'd be visited by professional shoplifters. The professionals usually confine their efforts to fast-moving new merchandise at stores. Also in your favor is the fact that some people who might steal from stores, rationalizing that the store can afford the loss, might not be willing to steal from an individual.

Nevertheless, police officials have found that there are people who attend many garage sales and are constantly stealing from them, making them at least semiprofessional thieves.

The first rule in protecting yourself is to be alert at all times. You don't have to follow people around and watch their every move. However, try to be aware of what's going on. Some shoplifters strike in the sale's early hours, when sellers are busiest. Especially watch people who dawdle for long periods in far-off corners for no apparent reason.

Another rule is to watch people who watch you. Most amateur shoplifters are self-conscious. Before pocketing an item, they'll keep glancing at the owner of the "store" to see if they're being observed.

There are also some other precautions that you should take. If you display merchandise in more than one room, try to have someone helping with the sale stationed in every room. If this isn't possible, put all easy-to-steal items in rooms that will be watched, and put bulkier pieces in other rooms. If you're selling items of considerable value, you should display them under lock and key, perhaps in a cabinet. If you're selling small, easy-to-conceal items, such as jewelry, it's a good idea to put them in or near your "command headquarters" so it will be easy for you to watch the display. If possible, display these items in a distinctive pattern—circles, X's, squares, or what-have-you—so it will be easy to see when an item is missing.

Don't Leave Your "Store" Unattended

Any time you leave your "store" unattended, you invite the possibility of theft. At least one person should be in the sale area whenever customers are present.

A common tactic used by shoplifters working in pairs or groups is for one to distract the seller while the others steal what they can. Any seller alone in a sale area should be on guard against this possibility. Another tactic is to lure the seller away from the sale area. In the case of garage sales, this is often done by sending someone to buy one or more bulky items. This person then asks for help to carry these items to a car, which may be parked some distance away. While the sellers are doing this, the buyer's confederates, perhaps hidden down the alley, hurry to the garage and steal as much as they can, probably beginning with the seller's cash box.

If you're alone, rather than leaving the sale area you could mark the item "sold," not moving it until help arrives or until the buyer returns with assistance.

How to Handle Shoplifters

If a shoplifter victimizes you, it's not likely that you'll catch him or her in the act. You probably won't notice that an item is missing until the thief has left, or the sale is over. Then you may recall that the last time you saw the item, it was being handled by someone. Often you'll be certain who stole the item, but will have no way of proving it.

The best way to handle people whose actions have made you suspicious is to begin devoting an excessive amount of attention to them. Follow them wherever they go; keep asking them what they're interested in, and if you can help them in any way. If they have larceny on their mind, they'll soon get discouraged and leave.

You must be on solid ground before actually accusing anyone of shoplifting. Merely being "sure" someone stole from you isn't enough. Unless you or someone helping with the sale actually saw the item being taken, it's always possible you made a mistake.

The laws of arrest are complex and vary from state to state. Law enforcement officers themselves often have a difficult time interpreting them correctly, despite their years of experience. As a private citizen, you should never even consider trying to physically detain a shoplifter unless the item you want to recover is of great value to you. Aside from the fact that you could be injured if the shoplifter resisted, you could be liable for criminal and civil charges if the courts found that you used "unreasonable force" in trying to detain someone. Ask yourself: Is it really worth the recovery of the item to take those legal and physical risks?

Police crime prevention experts suggest giving the shoplifter an "out" as a means of avoiding accusatory confrontations. Say something like: "Was that item yours, or something for sale?" Or, "I think you may have thought you already paid for that." This allows the thief to save face when caught, and not become aggressive. It also allows for the return of the item.

To be on the safe side, no matter what happens, you should *never* touch a shoplifter. If you see an item blatantly stolen, tell the suspect what you have seen and ask for the return of the item. If the shoplifter refuses, say you will call the police and ask the suspect to remain until the police arrive. If the shoplifter drives away before the police get there, try to get the license number of the suspect's car.

Again, chances are you won't have shoplifting problems. But if you encounter any, weigh the value of what was taken against the problems you could create by making a false accusation, or by getting involved in a physical altercation with the suspect.

Other Security Problems

If you live where crimes of violence are a constant threat, you shouldn't consider holding a garage sale under any circumstances. And even if you live in a "safe" neighborhood, you create potential hazards to yourself and your property any time you open your residence or any part of your property to strangers visiting your sale.

The most serious possibility is that of a crime against your person. This is not likely to happen when several customers are present, but when you are alone with just one customer it is always at least conceivable. That's why it's always a good idea to have at least one other person helping with the sale, especially if you are a woman or a senior citizen living alone. In any event, when alone with a customer who is capable of intimidating you physically, be especially alert.

Another potential hazard is burglary after the sale is over, inspired by something a would-be burglar or an accomplice may have seen when at your sale.

To reduce this risk, give customers as little opportunity as possible to learn that you own anything worth stealing. Don't allow strangers into any part of your home where they can observe valuables that are not for sale.

What Not to Sell

Whatever you do, don't try to sell anything suggesting that you are a serious collector of coins, stamps, fine jewelry, or other easy-to-carry valuables. If you want to sell fine jewelry, stamps, coins, silverware, or other items of considerable value, it would be safer to do so through an established dealer or an auction rather than trying to sell them to strangers who come to your home. As noted in Chapter 2, you'll probably get higher prices at those outlets anyhow.

Similarly, unless you live in a rural area where the ownership and use of firearms are commonplace, it would be prudent not to try to sell firearms of any age or condition at your garage sale, or to let it be known to visitors in any way that you own or collect firearms. Trying to sell books or magazines on firearms or gun collecting, for instance, would indicate that there are probably one or more guns in the house.

The Sale Begins— and You're on Your Own

On the night before the sale or early on the day the sale starts, get your outdoor signs up. (And if your sale runs more than one day, check them daily to be sure they're still up and in good condition.) Then put the finishing touches on your merchandise display.

As you can see, the secret of running a successful garage sale lies in the effort you're willing to put into getting ready for it. The more thorough your preparations, the easier and more successful your sale will be.

No matter how hard you try, you probably won't be completely ready when people begin showing up on the first day. The first arrivals will be there earlier than the time you advertised, and before you know it the sale will be going full swing. But if you've followed the advice in this book, at least you'll be pretty far along. You'll also be ready for some of the problems that may arise.

Once buyers begin pawing through your things, you're on your own. Those first few hours will be your busiest. And after those first few hours, you'll also be pretty far along toward being an "old pro" at holding garage sales.

You and Your Customers

If you've never dealt with the public before, your first sale will be an eye-opening experience. All sorts of people will show up. Most will be courteous and considerate, but there may be exceptions. Some people may be thoughtless; others may be careless and still others may be rude, perhaps commenting loudly that items are priced too high or otherwise badmouthing what you have to sell. The most boorish of them might even criticize your décor and/or your housekeeping.

Whatever they say, don't let it annoy you. Consider it part of your education into the mysterious workings of human nature.

Although this hardly ever happens, it's also conceivable that a visitor at your sale might become abusive or belligerent. If so, you have every right to politely ask the visitor to leave—and if the visitor refuses, to call the police.

Your own personality will go a long way toward determining how you'll handle your customers. Do what you feel most comfortable doing. If you've had sales experience, you don't need advice from this book; if you haven't, don't worry. Just use common sense.

In general, don't be standoffish or aloof. Try to make people feel at home. If someone seems especially interested in an item, tell him or her a little about it. You may clinch a sale that way. On the other hand, don't force yourself on people. Don't dog their footsteps and volunteer a lot of information they aren't asking for, or start quoting below-tag prices on items they've picked up merely to examine casually.

To put it another way, treat people at your sale the way you'd want to be treated if you went to someone else's sale.

They Won't All Buy

Accept cheerfully the fact that, for one reason or another, many people who come to your sale won't buy anything. Make them feel at home anyhow. Who knows? These people may be back later to buy, or may mention your sale to someone else who will drop in and take your biggest white elephant off your hands. No matter how uninterested people seem, give them a friendly "thanks for coming" as they leave.

Honesty Really Is the Best Policy

Trying to hide flaws in items you're trying to sell isn't just dishonest, it simply doesn't pay. By being honest with your customers you'll win their respect, not to mention your own self-respect. The flaws would probably be detected anyway—and by being honest you may sell more than you would otherwise.

Some sellers who ordinarily may be the most honest of citizens lose perspective when they hold a sale. They not only fail to point out serious flaws, they try to conceal them through such crude gambits as covering them with price tags. All you'll get with this kind of trickery is trouble. An angry buyer may return with an item later to demand his or her money back. No matter how graciously you handle that situation, your image will suffer. Potential buyers within earshot will be discouraged from buying anything themselves, and they will tell their friends and neighbors what they overheard.

All glassware, porcelain, fine art, etc., that you know is chipped, cracked, or otherwise flawed should have an "AS IS" notation on its tag. If appliances or other mechanical devices don't work properly, this should also be stated on the tag or told to potential buyers.

Learn as You Go Along

As your sale proceeds, you should be ready to make changes based on what you see and hear. For example, if there isn't enough room for people to move through your "aisles," clear a bigger space. If people are knocking items down or tripping over wires or other obstructions, get those things out of the traffic pattern.

If people are ignoring items because they're difficult to reach or see, make those items more accessible. If someone drawn by your sign says he or she almost missed your sale because the sign is too small or is hidden behind a tree, make a bigger sign or get your sign out in the open.

If a lot of people show up in the first hour or two but hardly anyone buys anything, your prices are probably much too high. Be ready at any time to review prices and lower those you conclude you innocently set at too high a level. Many sellers wait until the end of their sale to start lowering prices. The longer you wait, however, the less good this will do. Remember, the largest number of potential buyers will probably arrive at the beginning of your sale. If your sale spans several days, relatively few buyers may turn up in the final hours.

If your sale runs more than one day and your main motive for holding it is to clear out your closets or attic, consider cutting all of your prices in half on the final day.

When the Sale Is Over

When the sale is over, you'll be faced with the pleasant task of counting your money and the unpleasant one of putting everything you didn't sell back in storage. (Some people just throw out or give away their unsold merchandise.) If you took in a lot of money, it would be a good idea to deposit most of it in your checking or savings account as soon as possible.

One thing you should do immediately is to take down your sale notices and signs, especially your outdoor advertising signs.

This way you will avoid inconveniencing people who might see the signs and drive to the sale, not realizing that it is over. And you will be spared the inconvenience of unexpected and unwanted visitors hours or days after the sale has ended. Finally, it's just good manners. Occasionally weather-beaten signs remain posted on trees and telephone poles weeks after a sale, which hardly contributes to community beautification. If enough people did that, your local government might put onerous restrictions on the placement of all garage sale signs.

If you think you might hold another garage sale someday, sit down as soon as you can to write a critique. While the details are still fresh in your mind, sum up everything you learned during the sale and note what you'd do differently next time.

Note also what you observed about the effectiveness of your advertising. How did most people hear about your sale? Through your newspaper ads, your signs, word of mouth, or what? And note the price levels at which various categories of items seemed to sell best, as well as the types of items people seemed to want most and the types they ignored. Finally, file your critique away until your next sale, when you can take it out to refresh your memory.

Fund-Raising Garage Sales

Garage sales can be an effective way for small nonprofit groups and other organizations to raise funds. When these sales are held by such groups as Boy Scout and Girl Scout troops, senior citizen and special interest clubs, League of Women Voters chapters, local political parties, and similar organizations, they pose some special problems. However, they also offer opportunities for profit and promotion not available to people holding their own sales.

Selecting a Location

A small community group can hold a successful sale in a space volunteered by one of its members. The space might be somebody's garage or yard, or a porch or basement. But there are two other

73

options which may be better for larger groups, and which smaller groups may also wish to consider:

Holding your sale at several locations. If several members live near one another—or even better, on the same block, across the street from one another, or in adjoining homes—consider using all of these sites in your sale.

In addition to providing more sale space, this allows each garage, yard, porch, or other location to be used for various categories of merchandise. Put all the toys and games at one spot, all the clothes at another, all tools and appliances at another, etc.

Arranging to use someone else's space. Churches, fraternal or civic organizations, park districts or other local government bodies may give you free use of their property, or they may rent space to you.

Allow Much More Time

While it takes a lot of time to organize your own sale, it takes much more time to properly organize a group sale involving many volunteers, some of whom will be far more capable and conscientious than others. Therefore, a fund-raising group sale must be planned far in advance. Up to six months' preparation for a large sale isn't too much time. It may take that long to delegate responsibilities, make all group members aware of the sale, and give them time to tell their friends, relatives, and neighbors about it.

It's important to notify as many people as possible well in advance, so they'll start saving items for your sale that they otherwise might give or throw away. The more time your group's members and their friends and neighbors have to accumulate merchandise, the more merchandise you'll have to sell, and the more successful your sale will be. If you have many items, it will also take a lot of time to price and tag them. Don't wait until the last minute to begin. A pricing-and-tagging program for a big sale should start as much as a month or more before the sale. People could meet for an hour or two at a time to get the project well under way before the sale date.

Other Income Sources

In addition to merchandise donated by members and their friends, other income sources that small community groups can utilize are:

Consignment sales. Consider taking more expensive items on consignment from your group's members, and perhaps make it a condition of consignment that they work at the sale. To make it worthwhile, you should set a minimum price of at least $10 per item so your group won't be swamped with many low-price items that require cumbersome record keeping. For someone who consigns items and also contributes time to work at the sale, a fair commission would be 10 to 15 percent for your group.

For very expensive items, commissions can be negotiated. The people running one group sale got the seller of an upright piano to agree to a base price of $500—and then found a buyer at the sale willing to pay $700 for it, giving the group a $200 profit.

Bake sales. Bakery goods donated by members can be a big supplementary moneymaker. If it's a large sale, also consider selling candy and other snacks that children enjoy—and that will keep them occupied while their parents shop.

Arts and crafts. If you have a large sale, you can also supplement your income by allowing local arts and crafts people to have booths or tables at your sale, either for a fixed fee or for a percentage of their sales. If you don't know how to reach arts and crafts people, try press releases to your local newspapers.

Business donations. If your group is nonpartisan and has strong local support for its goals, you could also consider asking local merchants and business people for merchandise donations.

Assign Responsibilities

Whatever the size of your group, either an individual or a committee must be in charge, with the final say on all the questions that arise. In addition, responsibilities must be assigned for:

Merchandise collecting. Someone must take charge of collecting merchandise, storing it someplace before the sale, and getting it to the sale if it is stored at a different location.

Sign making and posting. Someone must oversee the preparation of signs and their placement in supermarkets and store windows, at strategic intersections, and along major streets and highways near the sale.

Supplementary income activities. These include consignment items, a bake sale, and merchandise donations from businesses.

Pricing. Some person or committee must set prices. Select people with the most experience in holding sales—or, if there are any in your group, individuals with some experience in the antique trade.

Tagging and marking. The bigger the sale, the more important it is to organize and begin these operations well in advance. Usually, items are priced as they are tagged.

Meals and/or snacks. If people working at the sale can't go home for lunch, someone should prepare or buy lunch for them—and prepare coffee and snacks during the sale.

Checking out buyers and handling money. If it's a big sale, this may require several people, at least in the sale's opening hours. And for security reasons, you should have at least two people in every sale area at all times anyhow. The person in charge should be responsible for seeing to it that you have enough coins and bills to make change when the sale starts. If your sale is held at more than one location—in several garages on the same block, for instance—you may also wish to set up a central cash-collecting procedure to assure that too much cash does not pile up at any location during the sale.

Advertising and publicity. Ads must be written and placed, and press releases prepared and distributed to local news outlets.

Two Special Problems

There are two problems unique to group sales. First, you have to decide what to do about group members who want to buy items donated by other members. This can be a delicate question, and it can lead to many disputes and misunderstandings if you don't establish a firm policy. Some groups give everyone who works on the sale the opportunity to buy a set number of items—usually no more than one or two—before the sale starts, at the price established by the pricing person or group. Whatever you do, it is essential to have a policy, and to make sure that everyone knows what it is.

Second, you must decide what to do with merchandise left over after the sale. You may sell it to members at greatly reduced prices, allow members to take what's left over for nothing, donate it to charity, or throw it out on the next garbage collection day. But establish this policy ahead of time too—and be sure everyone understands it.

Cut Prices as Your Sale Goes On

Because a fund-raising sale's goal is to raise as much money and clean out as much merchandise as possible, plan to cut prices in orderly fashion as the sale goes on. If it's a two-day sale, you could cut prices in half early on the second day, and in half again in the sale's final hours. Similar sales-stimulating methods are used at rummage sales held by churches and other groups. If some of your members have been involved in such sales, they may have some other suggestions.

Of course, if your sale includes consigned items, either they must be left out of the cost-cutting procedure, or consignors must agree to allow price cuts on their items.

Advertising and Publicity

As with your own sale, the fund-raising sale's advertising budget should be determined by how much you will have to sell. The bigger the sale, the more you should spend. If the sale is big enough, consider taking ads in more distant publications, or, in the case of groups in larger metropolitan areas, in classified columns of your major daily newspapers.

In addition, nonprofit groups holding sales should take advantage of opportunities for free publicity. Wherever you live, one or more local or community newspapers will probably carry stories about fund-raising garage sales for nonprofit groups. You may also have one or more local radio stations, or even a television station, carrying these announcements.

Announce your sale in a press release distributed to your local news media in plenty of time for it to be processed and used. To learn editorial deadlines of newspapers and radio and television newsrooms, phone or drop in and ask. Then submit your release several days before the deadline, to give the editor or news director plenty of time in which to schedule it.

Newspapers may also print weekly or monthly calendars of events that include sales held by nonprofit groups. Send your release to these departments too.

How to Write a Press Release

Your press release should be typed and double-spaced. If you are submitting it to local or community newspapers, have it delivered personally by the publicity chairperson or some other member of your group, preferably someone who knows the editor. Releases to more distant or large-metropolitan-area publications and editorial offices should be mailed.

If there is time and someone in your group has a good camera and knows how to use it, consider taking one or more pictures to be submitted with your press release. Typically these show people who will be working at your sale viewing some of the merchandise to be offered. But before spending time and money on photographs, phone or visit the newspaper editor to be sure the paper might use them, and learn the print size the paper might require. Picture captions should be fastened to the backs of the pictures with rubber cement, or you could type captions on removable labels and fasten them to the pictures.

Keep your press release simple but include all the essential details—where and when the sale will be held, the kind of items to be sold, the organization's name, and an explanation of what the organization does, if the name does not make that clear. If you wish, mention the names of people who helped organize the sale. Your release should always include the name and phone number of someone the editor or news director can call for more information.

If you do a reasonably good job of writing the release, some local and neighborhood newspapers will print it with little or no change. Other papers, especially most larger ones, rewrite virtually everything submitted to them.

On the facing page is an example of a short press release that includes all the essential facts about a group sale.

EVERYTOWN LEAGUE OF
WOMEN VOTERS
P.O. Box 2222
Everytown, IL
60068

FOR MORE INFORMATION
CONTACT:
Sue Bridges,
Publicity
345-4545

FOR IMMEDIATE RELEASE

LEAGUE OF WOMEN VOTERS TO HOLD "BLOCK GARAGE SALE"

The Everytown League of Women Voters will hold its third annual "block garage sale" from 9 a.m. to 5 p.m. Friday and Saturday (Sept. 5 and 6) in the 2400 block of West Riverside Drive.

Merchandise will be sold at four garages on the block and will range from toys, clothing, books, bric-a-brac, appliances, sporting goods, and general household goods to furniture, antiques, and collectibles.

Major items to be offered at the sale include an upright piano, several television sets, a grandfather clock, many sets of snow tires, and a camper.

Mary Cavanaugh, sale chairman, said there will also be a bake sale.

Sale committee members are Marge Friedman, Joan Jackson, Helen Schmidt, Elaine Rizzo, and Monique Petrowski.

15

Selling for Profit

Sooner or later, people who hold more than one garage sale may start thinking in terms of mixing some "for profit" items in with the usual run of household goods they're trying to dispose of. I'm not talking about professional or semiprofessional dealers who use house or garage sales to move merchandise acquired in the course of their business, or people with ready access to commercial merchandise sources through their family or friends. Instead, these are people with no previous contacts with the collectible or antique trade or other merchandise sources.

If you take this step, your garage sale will become a sideline business to some extent. At one extreme, you may include some "for profit" merchandise in sales you would have held anyhow, perhaps no more than once a year. At the other, there are people who buy as much for resale as they can, and hold as many sales as the traffic will bear. However active you become, it will also require your buying or otherwise obtaining the "for profit" merchandise.

Can You Really Make Money?

Is it really possible to make much money this way? Maybe. Everything is relative. No doubt some people do very well, although accurate information on this is difficult to obtain. For various reasons, some "for profit" sellers are very secretive about how well they are doing— and for reasons of vanity, others may greatly exaggerate their profits.

If you look at it purely on a dollars and cents basis, you'll probably net a lot less than you think. In calculating your "profit," you must also weigh the value of the time and effort spent buying merchandise and minding the store, not to mention the cost of the gasoline you'll burn looking for new things to sell, and the taxes on your profits.

With all these things figured in, most people will be better off viewing "for profit" selling at garage sales as a hobby rather than as a serious way to supplement their income. Still, a hobby that is at least potentially profitable makes more sense from an economic point of view than one that costs you a ton of money.

Other Things to Consider

Before getting too heavily involved with plans to sell for profit, here are some things to consider:

It could be illegal. If you plan to start holding more than just one or two sales a year, you could run afoul of local laws restricting the number of sales you are allowed to hold. Of course, if you have friends or relatives who would also like to sell for profit, you could get around those laws to some extent by combining merchandise and alternating sales among members of the group. In effect, you'd have a "floating" sale that moves from one location to another.

What about the neighbors? Even if there are no restrictions on the number of sales you can hold, consider what your neighbors might think about your holding a number of garage sales during the year, rather than just one or two.

Where will you put the stuff? If you get involved in buying many things for resale, you'll need someplace to store them between sales. Do you have the space? And are you (and others in your household) willing to put up with the inconvenience that might result? For instance, you might have so many things stored in your garage that you won't be able to fit your car in too.

Do Your Homework

If you start buying some items for resale, you should get serious about learning junque and antique values. This will enable you to avoid making costly buying mistakes and will help you recognize greatly undervalued items so you'll get fair prices for them.

In addition to visiting local antique shops and auctions, you should start reading some of the periodicals listed in Chapter 3. Also, invest in some pricing guides. Begin with one of the general guides listed in Chapter 3. Then, if you begin specializing in various categories of items, buy guides in those fields.

And beware of reproductions. So many antiques and collectibles are being reproduced today that even professionals are deceived. To protect yourself from paying antique prices for cheap reproductions, do as antique dealers do. Read as much about reproductions as you can, and start visiting gift shops and shows to see the latest items being reproduced. That way you'll recognize them when they start turning up at flea markets and small auctions.

Don't overlook discount and chain store gift departments, either. I can recall seeing a large drug chain in Chicago clearing out some red glass reproduction candy dishes, originally priced at 49¢ apiece, for two for a quarter. A few months later I saw dealers offering identical dishes at a big Texas flea market for $5 each.

The more serious you become about "for profit" selling, the more you may want to learn about the antique business. You'll probably get to know some of the dealers in your community, if you don't know them already. Cultivate these people if you can. You may even wish to sell them some of your better "finds," or to consign items to their shops if they accept consignments.

Becoming a Smart Buyer

To sell at a consistent profit, you must become a smart buyer. You must be much more hard-boiled about prices than when buying for your personal use or collection. Here are some buying tips:

Aim for big profit margins. Ordinarily, don't buy anything for resale unless you think you can get at least several times what you paid for it. This is a reasonable policy, because you won't always get as much as you hoped. You'll make mistakes and may even wind up with items you'll have to sell at a loss, if you can sell them at any price. Even people who have been in the trade for years make buying mistakes. There are so many categories of collectibles that it's impossible to keep up with all values.

Bargain, bargain, and bargain! When buying for resale, almost always be prepared to offer less than the asking price even though the asking price already assures you of a good profit. This goes for low-price items as well as expensive ones. Saving a dime or a quarter might not seem much by itself. But when you multiply this by the hundreds of small items you might purchase over the course of a year, it can add up to a lot of money.

When bargaining, however, always be polite. Treat sellers as you'd want buyers to treat you at your sale. Don't make insultingly low offers, and never contradict the seller or badmouth the merchandise. You'll never get a price concession that way, but you will make an enemy.

For big profits, think big. Always be alert for job lots you can buy at big discounts—assuming you have someplace to store the merchandise until your next sale. And if someone is selling many like items at a price so low you're sure you can resell them at a good profit, be ready to buy them all even if the seller makes little or no price concession.

Avoid damaged goods. Always inspect items carefully for chips, cracks, or other flaws. Other sellers may not be as conscientious as you are about marking such items "AS IS."

You'll also find many items offered at sharply reduced prices because they are damaged or chipped, but these are usually very bad "bargains." You may have to hold them for a long time before anyone will take them off your hands at any price. Unless you have the time and expertise to make professional repairs, anything you buy for resale should be in good condition.

Pay for Your Own Mistakes

Even though your goal is to make a profit, to keep your merchandise turning over you cannot charge more than the market will bear. Your prices on some items may be a little higher than if your motive was merely to clean out your basement or garage.

But whatever your motive, buyers still won't buy unless you provide real bargains. Your merchandise must still be priced to compete with that of other people holding garage sales in your community. If you find you paid too much for an item, don't expect someone else to pay for your mistake.

The worst thing you can do is fall into the trap of feeling that you "have to get your money back." Like a good poker player, when you see you have a losing hand, throw it in. And unlike the poker player, who must take a total loss, you can usually salvage something. Sell the item for whatever you can, and chalk the loss up to experience.

Retail stores do the same thing. When merchandise doesn't move, they keep cutting prices to whatever level *will* move it without regard to what it cost originally. The reason is to maintain what's called "cash flow." To put it another way, it's a lot better to have 50 percent of something than 100 percent of nothing. Then you can use that 50 percent to buy more merchandise, turn that over quickly at a profit, and use the proceeds to buy still more merchandise.

In selling for a profit, turnover is the name of the game. By turning merchandise over several times, you'll be dollars ahead of where you'll be if you wait in hopes that someone will finally come along and pay enough for you to get your money out of your "white elephants."

By the same token, don't fall in love with your merchandise. Some sellers like a piece so much that they ridiculously overprice it—supposedly to get a good profit, but actually to be sure nobody buys it and takes it away from them. If you like an item that much, be honest with yourself. Take it off the market and put it in your own collection.

Keeping Records

You may view the keeping of records of what you buy and sell as a nuisance, but the more serious you get about your "hobby" of reselling for profit at your garage sales, the sooner you start a good record-keeping system, the better. Good records will tell you if you're really making a "profit"—and what that "profit" is in relationship to the total amount of money invested in merchandise, no matter how small the scale of your operations.

To set up your records, list everything you buy, the date of purchase and the buying price, and give each item a stock number. Put the number on the item's tag. Then log the selling price and date when the item is sold. In other words, for good records, list *everything* sold at *every* garage sale you hold. To provide a more realistic picture of your "profit," you might also log the time you spend buying and selling merchandise, so you can calculate how much you are making per hour. Then calculate the cost of the gas used to buy and sell your merchandise.

If your "hobby" reaches the point where you are making actual profits, good record keeping becomes essential, because you will have a business on which you must pay taxes.

16

Where to Find Things to Sell

If one of your reasons (or the main reason) for holding a house or garage sale is to make a profit, you'll need sources of supply for what you sell. You or someone in your family may already own a store or have a relationship with someone who can supply you with new or used merchandise at below-market prices. But most people will have to start developing their own sources.

New Merchandise or Old?

Your first decision will be whether to concentrate on new merchandise, or on junque and other secondhand merchandise. All things being equal, you'll do better with used merchandise—the same mixture of items found at most garage sales. It costs a lot less to buy, and ordinarily your profit margins will be higher. At the same time, keep alert for opportunities to buy new merchandise at distress prices. Becoming aware of these opportunities is just a matter of training yourself to look for them.

Scrounging for Trash

A few regular garage and flea market sellers get some of their merchandise by scrounging for items other people have thrown away. Called "scavengers," they cruise streets and alleys looking for treasures among the garbage before the garbage collectors arrive. Some scavengers have furnished their homes with discards found this way. In fact, garbage collectors themselves are sometimes in the business. You'll find some at weekend flea markets, selling castoffs picked up during the week.

If you start cruising alleys looking for things to sell, it would be prudent not to offer anything found too near your home, unless you're sure the person who threw it out has moved away. It would be embarrassing to have the person who discarded the item see it for sale in your garage, and then loudly announce that to everyone within hearing.

Scrounging in alleys and garbage dumps isn't for everyone—and even hard-core scavengers don't go so far as to delve into trash bags and cans. Nevertheless, on the night before garbage pickup it's common to see scavengers cruising up and down alleys in cars and station wagons in many communities.

Before becoming an alley picker yourself, check local laws. In some communities it is illegal, although the law might not be actively enforced. Whatever the law, *never* step onto anyone's property. That's trespassing. Take items only if they are in the public alley, or in the parkway or street in front of the house.

While it's commonly believed that the best finds are in well-to-do neighborhoods, scavengers report that the opposite is often the case. People in more expensive homes are often the most aware of the value of their possessions, and they throw little of value away.

Other Garage Sales

Other garage sales can be your most productive sources of "for profit" merchandise for your own sales. Continually shopping other sales is also a good way to sharpen your knowledge of the current market and prices in your community. But don't buy something at every sale you visit just to be polite. As noted earlier, the commonest mistake most sellers make is to overprice merchandise. You may visit a number of sales before finding a single item you could be sure of reselling profitably at your own sale.

Shopping other sales requires a lot of self-discipline. You may spend a long time visiting other sales with little to show for it, and then you may come upon one or two sales that more than make up for that. Bargains will abound. One danger is that when you do find a sale with many bargains, you'll fail to take full advantage of the opportunity. Bargains will be so commonplace that you won't recognize them all.

You'll do best at sales where, for one reason or another, people are selling virtually everything and closing up a household. Obviously you'll find some of your best buys early in the sale, before many other buyers have had a chance to see the merchandise. You may also do well at the end, if sellers are in a mood to take big price cuts. Consider making offers for job lots or the entire remaining stock.

When buying at other garage sales, you may wish to do much of your buying at some distance from your own home, so buyers won't turn up at your sale and recognize their merchandise.

Flea Markets

Although flea markets are higher in the "junque and antique pyramid" than garage sales, a "for profit" garage seller can often find good buys for resale at them. You won't make many such purchases from experienced flea market dealers, even though they can make mistakes and undervalue merchandise too. And they may have bought some items at such low prices that they can afford to sell to you at prices low enough to allow you a decent resale profit. It's more likely that your best flea market buys will be from amateur and first-time sellers who are there primarily to clean out their attics and basements.

For the best flea market buys, get there as early as you can. Just as at garage sales, dealers and other knowledgeable buyers try to see as much merchandise as possible before anyone else does. By mid-morning, most of the best bargains will have been picked up by the pros.

Wear comfortable clothes and shoes, but don't dress up. Some flea market sellers ask higher prices of well-dressed buyers. Your equipment should include an umbrella, rain hat, sunglasses, magnifying glass, and a magnet (to help in identifying copper and brass—they won't attract it).

While there are many more amateur and semiprofessional dealers at flea markets than at antique shows, be careful. The quality of flea market merchandise is not as good, and there will be many more chipped and damaged items. Most of the merchandise at a flea market is priced for discount, so don't hesitate to bargain.

The bigger the flea market, the better it might be to start looking in the back and to work your way toward the more desirable locations in front. That's because at big markets, stalls conveniently located near the entrance are often occupied by professional dealers, who are least likely to have unrecognized bargains. The best buys are often found in the back and in the other hard-to-reach locations where amateurs usually wind up. Many flea markets assign space on a "first come, first served" basis, and amateurs are usually the last to arrive. In fact, some may still be arriving and setting up when you get there, giving you a chance to see their merchandise as it is being unpacked.

Other Merchandise Sources

Other possible sources of garage sale merchandise include:

Auctions. You may find some good resale buys at auctions. But to do so, you must be a highly disciplined buyer. It's easy to catch "auction fever" and wind up buying many items for much more than they are worth. You should get there early enough to view all of the merchandise before the auction starts. Never bid on an item unless you have examined it for chips, cracks, or other defects.

Some of the best resale buys may be job lots of junk, often sold by the box. But be sure you have a good idea of what's in the box before you bid.

Thrift shops. If you have the time and patience, you may uncover good resale buys at local junk and thrift shops. The best prospects are shops in neighborhoods or communities where major public works projects are under way and, for one reason or another, many people are moving.

Retail distress sales. True retail distress and "going out of business" sales can be sources of garage sale merchandise. Also, look for big discounts as stores clear out end-of-season merchandise.

Special outlets. Bigger cities have special outlets that sell new merchandise to flea market dealers and the like, and some of these companies also have mail-order operations. Some of them advertise in *Salesman's Opportunity Magazine*, Suite 1405, 6 N. Michigan Avenue, Chicago, IL 60602.

A problem with some of this merchandise is that it costs too much for profitable resale at garage sales. Also, if the same merchandise is being offered at local flea markets and by other "for profit" garage sellers, you will have to underprice it in order to move it.

Vacation trips. If you're traveling by car and have some extra space, some of your best resale buys may be found on vacation trips. Especially look for items not available near your own home that you can buy at bargain prices. This may be at garage sales, flea markets, or even retail souvenir and gift shops and stores.

Appendix A

House and Garage Sale Checklist

Things to Decide Before the Sale

Where will you hold your sale?
When will you hold it?
Will you hold it alone or jointly?
Will you take consignments? If so, on what basis?
Will you bargain for prices or hold firm?
How will you handle your money during the sale?
Will you accept checks or insist on all cash?
What kind of price tags will you use?
Where will you put your "command headquarters"?
Will you offer free coffee or other refreshments?
If "early birds" show up while you are preparing for your sale, will you let them in?

Things to Do Before the Sale

Market research:
> Visit other garage and house sales to check price levels and learn from other sellers.

Visit resale shops, antique shops and shows, etc., to see if any of your things are "collectible."

Visit your public library to see if it has pricing guides or specialized books on some things you plan to sell.

Place newspaper advertisements.

Place sale notices on bulletin boards, store windows, etc.

Clean up merchandise; make minor repairs.

Make signs for:

Outdoor advertising.

Point-of-sale information.

Get money for change before sale starts.

Price and tag merchandise.

Display merchandise.

Set up "command headquarters" equipped with:

Cash box.

Bags and newspapers, for wrapping.

Sign-making equipment, including signboards or white paper, scissors, markers, and transparent tape for fastening signs.

Things to Do After the Sale

Take down outdoor signs.

Take down advertising cards on bulletin boards, in store windows, etc.

Take cash to bank.

Write a postmortem if you plan to hold another sale.

Appendix B

Keeping Records for Joint and Consignment Sales

If you must keep records of joint or consignment sales, any system that works and is fully understood by all parties concerned will do, no matter how simple or complicated.

The following three systems are suggested only as a starting point. Any number of variations stemming from them are possible. The first two have the advantage of great simplicity. The third, for consignment sales only, is suggested primarily because it provides a complete list of consigned items. If the items are of some value, this would be a protection for both your consignors and you.

One of the simplest ways to keep records for a joint sale or consignment sellers is merely to rule off a column for each seller. Sellers tag their own items, identifying each tag with an initial or code number. Then list the items as each sale is made, either by price alone or by price and a description of the article.

Helen code H	Joan code J	Sue code S
lamp $4.00	table $4.00	bike $25.00
picture .50	book .25	bottle $1.00
dishes .25	typewriter $15.00	vase $2.00
clock .75		

Another simple system is to have sellers or consignors tag their own items with coded, removable tags. Then, as each item is sold, remove the tag and paste it to the "sold" sheet under the seller or consignor's name. If you use this system, someone in the selling group must be given the responsibility of removing the tag from each item as it is sold.

Helen code H	Joan code J	Sue code S
H $4.00	J 4.00	S $25.00
H $14.00	J 25¢	S $7.00
H 75¢	J 15.00	S $2.00

If you want a record of all the items brought to you by consignors, have them provide you with a list. They must also tag their items, identifying tags with code numbers keyed to their lists. For instance, if a consignor's code letter is "H," the consignor lists and tags items as "H–1," "H–2," etc.

Using this system, you can check out each item on the list when the lot is brought to you by the consignor, to be sure all merchandise is actually received. Then you check items out as they are sold. If you wish, you could also make a notation on the list when you pay a consignor for a sold item.

The advantage of this system is that it puts the burden of preparing the list and tagging items entirely on the consignor. However, its effectiveness depends on the consignor's ability to draw up a legible and workable list.

Consignor Helen - Code letter H				
Item no.	Description	Price	Sold	Paid Helen
H-1	oil lamp	$4 00	✓	✓
H-2	picture	.50		
H-3	set of dishes	6 00		
H-4	red glass vase	1 00	✓	
H-5	typewriter	15 00		
H-6	raincoat	2 00		